BJ67 M

LYNDON JOHNSON

THE TRAGIC SELF

A Psychohistorical Portrait

LYNDON JOHNSON
THE TRAGIC SELF

A Psychohistorical Portrait

Hyman L. Muslin, M.D.
and
Thomas H. Jobe, M.D.

With a Foreword by
Allan W. Lerner, Ph.D.

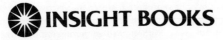 **INSIGHT BOOKS**

PLENUM PRESS • NEW YORK AND LONDON

Library of Congress Cataloging-in-Publication Data

Muslin, Hyman L., 1929-
    Lyndon Johnson : the tragic self : a psychohistorical portrait /
  Hyman L. Muslin and Thomas H. Jobe ; with a foreword by Allan W.
  Lerner.
       p.   cm.
    Includes bibliographical references and index.
    ISBN 0-306-43763-5
    1. Johnson, Lyndon B. (Lyndon Baines), 1908-1973--Psychology.
  2. Presidents--United States--Biography.   I. Jobe, Thomas.
  II. Title.
  E847.2.M87   1991
  973.923'092--dc20
                                                            91-210
                                                            CIP

This book is a work of interpretation applied to the large body of documentary material on the life of Lyndon Johnson. Our intention has not been to sift through the material we have examined as to its validity, that being the mission of the historian, not, in our view, of the psychohistorian. Our endeavor has been to gain an understanding of Lyndon Johnson through the lens of psychoanalytic self psychology.

ISBN 0-306-43763-5

© 1991 Plenum Press, New York
A Division of Plenum Publishing Corporation
233 Spring Street, New York, N.Y. 10013

An Insight Book

History teaches that among the men who have overturned the liberties of republics, the greatest number have begun their career by paying obsequious court to the people; commencing demagogues and ending tyrants.

ALEXANDER HAMILTON,
The Federalist (1787–1788)

The great act of faith is when a man decides that he is not God.

OLIVER WENDELL HOLMES,
Letter to William James, 1907

FOREWORD

The psychologically tinged biographical study of a political figure is no longer a rarity. However, psychologically sophisticated studies of political figures are rare. Indeed, learned depth psychological studies of such subjects are rarer still. Rarest of all is the psychobiography that rises to the level of truly applied psychoanalysis, that employs the conceptual model of a new and exciting school of psychoanalytic theory in a fashion that elucidates theory itself in the course of probing its subject. Drs. Muslin and Jobe have written such a book.

Sophisticated and articulate representatives of the Kohutian self psychology school of psychoanalysis, the authors suggest an intriguing perspective on Lyndon Johnson's inner life and its relationship to his actions. In doing so, they manage to offer something new and provocative in the understanding of a political figure and an era which have been analyzed and agonized over unremittingly.

Scholars interested in depth-psychology perspectives on politics will find in this book a highly adaptable, parsimonious, and elegant conceptual scheme for exploring both the healthy and pathological aspects of relationships between leaders and followers, on both the mass and small-group scales. The self-psychology concepts of the nuclear and completed selves, the dynamics of self–selfobject relations, the reciprocal character of self and group self as organizing concepts in the study of leader–follower relations, the reinterpretation of the concept of fixation in the context of self maintenance, the individual and collective manifestations of narcissistic rage and fragmentation of the self, the relevance of the experiences of leadership and followership to the maintenance of adequate self-functioning in some personality types—all these valuable concepts and more are theoretically integrated, clearly explicated, and suggestively illustrated in this book.

As befits a healthy and significant theoretical school, psychoanalytic self psychology will undoubtedly continue to offer extensions and refinements of its conceptual matrix and clinical precepts. It is to be no less expected as part of this process that its distinct approach should be correspondingly extended to the subject matter of applied psychoanalysis. This latest volume by Drs. Muslin and Jobe is a fascinating contribution to that process.

ALLAN W. LERNER
Professor of Political Science and Associate Dean of the Graduate College
University of Illinois at Chicago
Chicago, Illinois

ACKNOWLEDGMENTS

We wish to express our gratitude to several people who have been of service to us throughout our work in producing this book. We wish to offer our appreciation to our wives, Bernice and Patricia, and to our children, Anthony, Suzanne, Elizabeth, and William. They all offered the steady infusion of support vital to our cohesion. Our secretaries, Barbara Edwards and Carol Kimsey, were of great help in the preparation of this work.

We also would like to express our gratitude to Norma Fox, executive editor of Insight Books, for her consistent concern with our words and with our psychological equilibrium.

We are indebted to our colleagues and students at the University of Illinois, especially in our workshop on Literature and Psychology. The contributions of Drs. Marcus Wigutow and Bahwani Prasad are particularly appreciated.

A special note of thanks to Dr. Arnold Goldberg, president of the Chicago Psychoanalytic Institute, for his encouragement and steady support in the preparation of this book.

We also want to offer a special gesture of appreciation to our mentors who have made an impact on our thinking and shaped our interest in the areas of history and psychoanalysis: Heinz Kohut, Lester King, and Allen Debus.

Finally, we wish to acknowledge with gratitude permission to quote from the following sources:

Robert A. Caro, *The years of Lyndon Johnson: The path to power.* New York: Knopf. Copyright © 1982 by Alfred A. Knopf, Inc.

George Christian, *The President steps down.* New York: Macmillan. Copyright © 1970 by the Macmillan Publishing Company.

Doris Kearns, *Lyndon Johnson and the American dream.* New York: Harper & Row. Copyright © 1976 by Harper & Row, Publishers, Inc.

CONTENTS

INTRODUCTION

by *Lawrence Z. Freedman, M.D.**

> *All men are born politicians and some never grow out of it.*
> —H.D. Lasswell

Drs. Muslin and Jobe have written a powerful psychological study of such a man as Lasswell describes, Lyndon Baines Johnson. This psychological analysis of the thirty-sixth president of the United States contains an historical search. The investigation reflects man's ancient and persistent effort to understand his leaders, their powers, and their vulnerabilities. This contemporary effort is enriched by the extraordinary ubiquity and penetration of modern media. In democracies, the scope, access, and technology to observe and report on the present behavior and lifelong development of presidents is unprecedented. The massive detail and documentation are here creatively employed to integrate self

*Professor Emeritus of Psychiatry, University of Chicago, and Chairman, Institute of Social and Behavioral Pathology.

1

psychology and the man who led this country during its most divisive conflict since the Civil War.

As we read this fascinating account, we are struck with the historical and even mythological parallels between leaders over time. Herodotus described Scyles, king of the nomads, and the diffuse traditions of his subjects. His Hellenistic mother taught him Greek language, culture, and values. The internalized conflict between his father's simple culture of origin and his mother's Greek ideal ultimately destroyed him. Sophocles dramatized the tragedy of Oedipus and Euripides, the poignant dilemma of Antigone, forced to choose between the demands of filial fidelity and responsibility to the state demanded by her uncle Creon. From Sophocles' Oedipus came Freud's psychoanalytical construct of the inborn dilemma of man, projected onto his parents.

Freud was no stranger to the analysis of political figures. On October 24, 1928, H.D. Lasswell, a guest of Freud's Vienna Psycho-Analytical Society, delivered a paper entitled "Can We Distinguish Different Types Amongst Politicians and Is Their Taking Up Politics Conditioned by Certain Definite Factors in Themselves?" Lasswell, my erstwhile colleague, founder of policy science, believed and wrote that "damaged self-esteem" is a probable cause of "power needs." Two years later, in 1930, Freud collaborated with American diplomat William C. Bullit on a psychological study of Woodrow Wilson, twenty-eighth President of the United States, who led the Allied powers during World War I, in which Freud's sons were fighting for the opposing Axis armies. Freud found another tragic president, another narcissistic deficit preserved into an adult political life in which, as a president with many significant achievements, Wilson was, so Freud believed, incapable of achieving satisfaction in any success short of "saving the world."

Beginning in 1914, Freud developed his analyses of Moses, the molder of the Jewish group consciousness, purveyor of its values, and penultimate creator of its political and national being. He was, Freud was convinced, not a Jew but a dissident Egyptian noble.

Schraeber, senate president of the highest court in Saxony, was a major political contemporary of Freud's, whose autobiography, written during his paranoid psychosis, provided Freud with the empirical platform for his theory of the origin of paranoia as a product, in part, of repressed homosexuality.

Assassination brought Vice President Lyndon Johnson to the presidency on November 23, 1963, when young President John F. Kennedy was assassinated in Texas, Johnson's home state. Dubbed "the accidental president," resented as the successor to his admired and martyred predecessor, Johnson achieved much but tragically left the presidency, believing he had failed.

A century earlier, the assassination of President Lincoln brought Vice President Andrew Johnson to power. National violence, the Civil War in the nineteenth century, the Vietnam War in the twentieth century, and the murder of a president perfused the perception and experience of each leader. Each was southern, less educated than his advisers, but endowed with the natural force of powerful intellect. Each was sensitive and defensive about his lack of polish and education. Andrew Johnson was the only president ever to have been impeached; Lyndon Johnson felt driven from office by the powerful passions engendered by a divisive war.

Johnson was a gigantic man, one of the most effective leaders the United States has produced in the twentieth century. His achievements in human rights are historic. His goals for social and economic reform were great, in their ideals and in their legislation, which he propelled. Gigantic, too, was his pursuit of victory in the war in Vietnam.

Johnson was brilliant, energetic, and dedicated. His achievements and his failures were monumental. His political persona and his personality as perceived in the press and television were baffling and exasperating, intriguing and inspiring, to the American public.

Johnson was a mythological figure in the sense that he symbolically reflected and distorted the reality of himself, of his political leadership, and of the polis which he led. During his presidency, we saw only the secondary reflection of the man and the leader. The childhood of this "heroic" figure, like those in mythology, endured long periods of obscurity and saw Johnson in extreme danger of disgrace. He showed extraordinary capacity; he had been required to face and survive. There were anecdotes of precocious strength, cleverness, and wisdom. In myths, the hero as warrior slays the monster of the status quo. The hegemony wrested from the enemy, the freedom won from the malice of the monster, the life energy released from the toils of the status quo, is symbolized in women.

The feelings, insights, and constructs of self psychology are integrated into what has been reported of the earlier development, within his family of origin, his infancy, childhood, adolescence, and youth, and his emergence as the leader of the world's most powerful nation during the era which followed World War II.

With stunning clarity this analysis demonstrates

that the self-deficits of Johnson, the extraordinary unmet need for approval, and the fear of loss of self-worth affected his presidential decisions. The social programs of the Great Society and the extraordinary expansion of the Vietnam War, decisions made to protect his own very vulnerable sense of self-worth, became the fate of the nation and of the world.

The expository and analytic power of self psychology is extraordinary because it is particularly powerful in studying the leader and the community over which he presides. The earliest intrapsychic needs are analyzed and followed as the self develops. The infant and small boy become the leader who could affect the lives of millions.

What is the value of this psychological exposition of a great political leader in a democracy? The authors express the hope that this example of the relevance of intrapsychic mechanisms to prediction of leadership decisions becomes increasingly a part of the electoral scrutiny in a democratic society of candidates for office. The problems are as great as the promise, but we are persuaded by this dialectic between presidential leadership and neonatal experience. Thesis and antithesis resulting in the dialectic synthesis of the political leader are instruments of perception and political prediction which the individual citizen and the voting public in a great democracy should, indeed must, include in their evaluation of the decision of who should be chosen.

Chapter 1

THE MISSION OF THE BOOK
TOWARD A PSYCHOLOGICAL
PORTRAIT OF LYNDON B. JOHNSON

The goal of this book is to present a psychological portrait of Lyndon Baines Johnson, the thirty-sixth president of the United States and arguably the most vilified of all American leaders, including Abraham Lincoln. Although Ulysses Grant was denounced as "the drunken Democrat whom the Republican dragged out of the Galena gutter," and Lincoln was variously labeled as the "Illinois ape or baboon, satyr, buffoon" (Mooney, 1976, p. 189), no president was subjected for so long to the hatred of outraged citizens whose chants taunted: "Hey, hey, LBJ, how many kids did you kill today?"

Perhaps the most frequent more detached description of Johnson as a unique personality was that he was multidimensional. A veteran Johnson aide and biographer wrote of this aspect:

> He was an entire cast of characters: bulldozing ambitious politician, sentimental family man, Mr. Vanity, frustrated schoolmaster, locker room raconteur, hardheaded business-

7

man, Uriah Heep, journalism instructor, paternalistic employer, moody self-analyst, friend in time of need. (Mooney, 1972, p. 276)

To be comprehensive, this list of Johnson's myriad personalities must include immobilization by ineptitude and fear of failure; chronic fears of the "enemy"—usually Bobby Kennedy—or the "intellectuals" who might find a soft spot in him to attack; his incapacity to share his emotional neediness with anyone, coupled with the need to maintain a vigilant posture of the grandiose self toward his surround. There is the inability to "self-calm," to subdue his agitation, manifest in the constant activity, usually described as his enormous *energy*; the painful and feared states of emptiness and loneliness; the lack of self-worth, coupled with his insistence on always being the victor, holding center stage, and thereby the admiration of others; his sycophancy evident from adolescence, toward sources of power; the absence of a fixed constellation of values, which permitted him to ally himself with various and sometimes opposing groups and sources of power without experiencing shame or guilt (Caro, 1983; Kearns, 1976; Johnson, 1969; Evans & Novak, 1966; Goldman, 1969; Mooney, 1973; Steinberg, 1968).

Our goal is to illuminate the essence of the *self* of Johnson, to explore his background, and then to identify how much of his adult interactions reflected his early influences, especially those involving his childhood caretakers.

Psychological analysis offers a view of the *dynamic, genetic,* and *adaptive* forces within the person. These various points of view of the psychological approaches to understanding are necessary to (1) understand the ongoing or operational intrapsychic core of vulnerabilities and deficits and the attempts to achieve a cohesive self (the *dynamic* point of view); (2) understand the developmental influences—positive and negative—that shaped the adult self (the *genetic* point of view); and (3) distinguish, through empathic observations, the behavior that is a response to represent "archaic" threats—those no longer present or effective—from behavior that is a response to current circumstances (the *adaptive* point of view).

A volume devoted to a psychological version of a person should offer a *model of the mind*—a method by which to understand the scrutinized subject. It then should collate the available data so as to make the subject understandable to us. This latter enterprise is especially compelling in the study of Lyndon Johnson. How can we understand a Lyndon Johnson who, cloaked in power, quailed at the barbs of a former opponent (Robert Kennedy) who at that moment in history was not in office? How can we understand the self-enfeeblement that deterred Johnson from running for the presidency in 1960? Or that made him fear standing for election in 1964 at the height of his popularity? How do we understand his penchant for demeaning those under his command in order to buttress his role as leader when he was surrounded by instruments of power and manifestations of his worth? Finally, how can we gain some understanding of the man, as leader, who could not empathize* with those who were separated from their

*We are using the words *empathy* and *empathize* to indicate the cognitive understanding of another person's inner world of thoughts and feelings. The term empathy in this sense is distinct from identification, a term reserved for the process in which a person develops a similar feeling or a mental state by accretion and distinct from sympathy in which a person experiences compassion for another.

families and exposed to harm or death? Indeed, repeated decisions made throughout the recorded lifetime of this man reveal an utter absence of empathy where his self-needs were to be considered.

It seems clear that an understanding of Johnson can only be sought through the lens of an in-depth exploration of his inner self by the use of materials that form valid data bases.

The psychological student of historical figures uses the same data, of course, as any other researcher, with crucial distinctions. The psychological investigator is not only interested in the recorded factual material. He probes those facts as elements of a sequence of behaviors revealing tendencies, vulnerabilities, or responses to intrapsychic events. These include reactions to disappointments or insults which resulted in particular actions.

The psychological investigator scrutinizes interviews between the primary subject and others which reflect the self of the primary subject exhibited at that time, and with that particular interviewer. Who was the Johnson whom Jack Valenti knew? Whom Dean Rusk knew? Whom Doris Kearns knew?

While none of the observations made during interviews were set down for the purpose of creating a psychological portrait, the psychological investigator will be able to "see" a facet of Johnson which might escape the ordinary observer. Johnson could and did posture as whatever self would best gain the gratifications he sought at a particular time with a particular source.

Perhaps the central criterion that differentiates the systematic inquiry performed by an investigator of history from that in psychotherapy is that the psychotherapist ultimately communicates his "findings" to his *patient.* His hope is confirmation of his hypotheses through release of disavowed or repressed remembrances, or through symptom reduction. We cannot obtain such confirmations from Lyndon Johnson. Yet what we seek to perform is essentially a case study.

The "model of the mind" which we utilize here to comprehend Lyndon Johnson is derived from psychoanalytic self psychology. Self psychology is concerned with the self as the center of mental life. It encompasses the individual's experiences of his drives, his assertiveness, his ideals, and his talents and skills. In the view of self psychology, not only is the self the center of the psychological universe; the *maintenance of its cohesion* is the crux of mental health. This is in contradistinction to the schema of classical psychoanalysis, where it is the balance of forces between the drives and their defenses and the resolution of conflicts, especially the oedipal conflicts.

In the view of self psychology, "Tragic Man"—the individual preoccupied with gaining inward "succor" for his "depleted" self—replaces "Guilty Man"—the individual preoccupied with the avoidance of oedipal guilt—as the overriding problem in Western civilization.

The complete self is conceived of as a supraordinate structure: a receiver of impressions and a center of action. A complete self has two major constituents: (1) one pole from which emanates the basic strivings for power and success, the pole of ambitions; and (2) another pole which is the seat of the basic idealized goals of this self, the pole of ideals.

The development of the pole of ambitions is initiated through special activities of the parent who functions as an admirer, approver, or echoer of the unfolding self. These are the mirroring functions of the parent.

From the viewpoint of the child, this parent is experienced as an entity over whom the child has total control, much as one controls various parts of one's body. Hence the designation *"selfobject"*; or, in this case, the *"mirroring* selfobject." Over time, the dyad between the infant self and its mirroring selfobject, the "archaic" *self/selfobject fusion,* is replaced by the self internalizing the selfobject functions. Thus selfobject mirroring is replaced by *self-esteem;* a mother's applause, over time, becomes the experience of self-worth.

At about the same time in an infant's self development, the second major influence on its self growth occurs. The *"idealized parental imago selfobject"* is established. Selfobjects are to be sharply differentiated from objects in psychoanalytic theory. Objects are thought of as discrete from the self. They never fuse with the self as selfobjects. *Objects* may be human, nonhuman, or symbolic. They are always sought after (or repelled) by virtue of their unique qualities. The falling-in-love with a human object reflects a unique attractiveness to a particular self, rather than for the selfobject *functions* of providing *"mirroring,"* or *"calming."*

Thus a selfobject relationship may be formed with no awareness of the selfobject's uniqueness as a person. An *object* relationship is one in which the object is prized for his or her special features, not for selfobject—and essentially anonymous—functions of *"mirroring"* or *"calming."* The idealized parent imagoes are figures whom the child looks up to, and merges with, as an imago of calm, soothing, perfection, and thus as a source of perduring strength. Once the functions of the archaic idealized parent imago are interiorized into the self, the self is in possession of its own resources for control, for self-calming and self-soothing, as well as of a pole of ideals.

Self/selfobject relationships form the essence of psychological life, from birth to death. The nature of this relationship changes over time, and in functioning. From the archaic selfobject relationships, there is a developmental line of self/selfobject encounters to what is called the mature selfobject relationships. These offer an experience of empathic resonance: the support of a colleague through which the adult self can experience a revival of the memories of the archaic selfobject's mirroring, or direction.

The position of self psychology with regard to psychopathology is that *all* its forms ultimately derive from defects in the overall structure of the self, or from distortions of the self. Both are due to disturbances of self/selfobject relationships in childhood. In childhood, a failed self/selfobject relationship by both the mirroring selfobject—the admirer and echoer of the unfolding self—and the idealized parental selfobject—the calmer, and soother, and direction-giver—will result in a self *depleted* of "self-worth," and "self-calming."

This self will be highly vulnerable to insults and disappointments. It will feel a pervasive sense of emptiness and loneliness. This self will experience great difficulty in forming permanent bonds based on the unfolding of needs for admiration, calming, and direction, reflecting anxieties toward allowing any self/selfobject bonds to form.

Another common phenomenon in persons with these self deficits is to become immersed in transitory relationships in which an archaic self/selfobject dyad is formed and then is rejected due to a mixture of anticipated disillusionment because the relationship cannot offer them the longed-for childhood gratification. These self disorders, emanating from failures in the development of the self in childhood, come about when the primary mirroring selfobject has failed, and is not compensated by the idealized parent selfobject in promoting the required self-esteem to maintain a cohesive self.

An important aspect of the clinical theory of psychoanalysis and psychoanalytic self psychology is that of the *transference*. Transference refers to the investment onto current human figures of the qualities of archaic figures from the past. A person in a *"selfobject mirroring transference relationship"* with his spouse experiences his wife as if she were the embodiment of his mother's mirroring functions. In their relationship he petitions for mirroring gratifications.

Another aspect of the transference is the concept of *defense* transference. Here the subject experiences the current human figure as an embodiment of his archaic selfobject, who is feared or hated, and defends himself against this transference figure. Lyndon Johnson was one who entered into many transference and defense transference relationships throughout his life.

The insights of self psychology are of value in the fields of history and social sciences, especially in understanding the formation, maintenance, and disruptive processes of groups. One of the applications of self psychology to problems in history is that of the concept of the group self. The group self is analogous to the individual's self. A group self includes the central ambitions and the ideals that characterize the group in its ordinary operation. An important source for maintaining the integrity of any particular group is the leader needed or chosen by the group in various situations, especially in circumstances of impending fragmentation, the result of any self/selfobject rupture or group self/selfobject rupture.

Self psychology thus far has identified two types of leaders, although many combinations exist. In the first type, the *messianic leader* is the embodiment of rectitude, the fusion between the self and its pole of ideals. These personalities set themselves up as the perfect leader, worthy of reference. An example of this type of leader was Adolf Hitler, who effected a repair of the German group self in its experience of ineptitude after World War I. The second type, the *charismatic leader,* has become one with his pole of assertiveness, and thus experiences and exudes omnipotence and certitude. Winston Churchill was such a leader, needed by the British people during their crisis of survival in World War II, and abandoned when the need for an omnipotent leader was at an end.

In later sections of this book (Chapters 5 and 6), the application of these principles of self psychology will be utilized to collate the data we have gathered to penetrate the complexities of the self of Lyndon Johnson and the group self/selfobject dyad he formed with the group self of the American people.

The final mission of this volume is to offer a psychological model for understanding the selves of those who seek positions of leadership, so that a psychologically enlightened electorate populace can, with adequate information, discern those who are best qualified to lead.

We then proceed from a version of *what* Lyndon Johnson was as a psychological being to a description of the sources of *his* early influences, to the final understanding of the particular interactions and behaviors he exhibited in adulthood that represented needs derivative of past conflicts and vulnerabilities. Finally, the volume will focus on the Vietnam war and Johnson's involvement in this period in America's history which directly reflected his self-needs.

We now enter into a study of Johnson as he appeared to colleagues, family, and friends in his adult years.

Chapter 2

THE MANY SELVES
OF LYNDON JOHNSON

Here we concern ourselves with the self, or selves, of Lyndon B. Johnson as presented to those who were his allies, mentors, nurturers, competitors, love or sex objects, confidants and, at times, victims.

The methodological approach of this chapter is to gather versions ("selves") of Lyndon Baines Johnson as he was experienced by people with whom he interacted. This documentation of his various selves will, when synthesized, render a portrait of the central (nuclear, cohesive, or prominent) self of Johnson, and the different selves he became to serve his moment-to-moment needs for self-gratification or self-repair.

Johnson was complex—the conventional euphemism for a person who exhibits many different selves reflecting needs on differing (and varied) developmental levels. That is, he had various *fixations* of his self which he demonstrated through his lifelong attempts to structure interactions so as to reenact earlier ones. He drew archaic gratifications from these interactions of duplication.

Some interactions he unconsciously structured to yield the instant, reflexive, applauding of a parental object: the mirroring function of an empathic parent recognizing the infant and youngster's need to achieve the requisite experience of worth. In other interactions which he structured consciously and unconsciously, he became the fawning receptive youngster wide open to direction, and to the calming and soothing that derive from a trusted leader with whom one can merge. In yet another form of relationship Johnson and a significant other matched each other in many respects and he thereby reduced his sense of aloneness.

Johnson also formed relationships with different persons in which *he* was the leader—the nurturer or commander, or the tyrant or mentor. To his aides, he *was* the idealized parent, akin to an emperor, whose commands were not to be challenged. His leadership was often expressed in malevolent behaviors, such as insults, irrational dismissals, and invasions of their privacy (e.g., checking their files after office hours). Of course, his so-called leadership and domination of others covered other needs in Johnson, as was revealed whenever anyone threatened to leave his employ. Johnson would sulk, insult the employee and future employer, and do whatever was calculated to force the employee to give up the idea of leaving (Christian, 1940; Mooney, 1976; Reedy, 1970).

In all of these encounters, Johnson was never able to be gratified—sufficiently calmed or sufficiently celebrated—so that one could state that with his wife, or with his mother, or with Sam Rayburn, he was at *peace*. Another facet of his psychic world was an unremitting striving to be the central player in each of the many types of interactions in which he became engaged, whether he was in his self of servitude, or of leadership.

A further aspect of his hostile leadership was his difficulty—in reality, his inability—to apologize when one of his commands or positions was found to be inaccurate or invalid. No one ever heard Lyndon Johnson admit being wrong or inept. Even after having been proved wrong, he could not endure being in error and the consequent loss of self-worth (Sam Houston Johnson, 1969). The domination he exerted over his dominion—from the ties his male aides wore, to the amount of lipstick his wife used, to the papers left on desks—which he scrutinized after aides and secretaries went home—was so sweeping that it gave his people a sense of being an instant member of his family. In Johnson's family, however, all the members—aides, wife, children—worked for him. Johnson was on everyone's case, constantly hounding, constantly exhorting his army to work harder, even though he paid them relatively little. One observer even noted that Johnson's aides all walked in that same hustling gait that he called "the Johnson trot" (Reedy, 1970).

Johnson also had many relationships with people who were his peers and with whom he experienced camaraderie—mutuality of empathy, in a twinship type of bond. But the interactions were most commonly directed to a specific goal of his, such as a favor either needed or given. These friends ranged from high school and college mates, to members of the Congress, to friends he acquired when he became a power in Congress. Often these "friends" were people to whom he revealed his specific needs of the moment.

Thus, in each interaction, Johnson betrayed his needs to acquire, from each encounter, no matter what

form it took, narcissistic "supplies" for the establishment and/or maintenance of his self-cohesion.

Finally, the Johnson story has been chronicled by a
mix of observers writing from a distance; reporters
(Dugger, 1982; Evans & Novak, 1966) who knew him as
journalists "know" their subjects; writers who knew
him through a scholarly investigation of documents, or
from interviews of people who had contact with him
(Caro, 1983; Halberstam, 1972; Steinberg, 1968); and a
set of scribe-confidants (Kearns, 1976; White, 1964).

We now pursue the major thrust of this chapter:
examination of the experiences and reactions of a number of those with whom Lyndon Johnson interacted —
his wife, mother, aides, advisers, colleagues, reporters,
and others to whom he turned for infusions of worth,
calming, and direction — his personal pantheon of idealized figures. By collating the various printed expres-
sions of their involvement with Johnson we arrive at an
answer to our initial research query: What made up the
self of Lyndon Johnson?

The answer to this question represents an empathic
diagnosis and a model of the self of Lyndon Johnson.
This composite self-model will comprise the special
quality of his strivings for object (i.e., a unique separate
self valued for its own qualities) and selfobject gratification; his self-vulnerabilities; his self-defenses, especially his defenses against any show of ineptitude, such
as grandiosity; and his need to protect himself against
bonding with people, as well as his fear of loneliness.

JOHNSON AS SELFOBJECT

There was of course a large group of people for
whom Lyndon Johnson was the center of the universe.

Their writings present Johnson as hero, Johnson as the
source of worth, Johnson as the perpetual leader to be
followed and worshiped, and Johnson the leader who
was revered and despised. Michael Davie (1966), the
foreign correspondent, captured an experience of this
type:

> The President comes into a room slowly and warily, as if
> he means to smell out the allegiance of everyone in it. He is
> big, a hulking six feet three, and despite a definite paunch and
> the recurrent anxieties about his health, he looks like a man
> with exceptional physical stamina. Here, the "complexity," in-
> deed, the contradictions in the man, are rendered in his physi-
> cal presence: There is a faint air of the barroom strategist. The
> face is unprepossessing. The ears are huge, with long hanging
> lobes; the brow is a mass of complicated furrows; the mouth is
> a straight line. He dresses like a man who has told the best
> tailor in town to fit him out like a pillar of the Chamber of
> Commerce. When he shakes your hand (his own hand is ca-
> pacious, hard, and brown, with a long vein down the back), he
> gives you the politician's sincere look straight between the
> eyes. His manner is restrained. His voice usually is very quiet,
> with a pronounced Southern accent, saying "strawng" for
> "strong." Afterward, you chiefly remember the small eyes,
> steady and unrelenting under half-lowered lids. (p. 3)

In contrast, Jack Valenti (1975), a top aide to Johnson
as president, glorified Johnson:

> Once during the deadly days of the Nazi terror, when
> France had been overrun and the heel of the Nazi was on the
> neck of the French, Winston Churchill spoke to the French
> people: "*Français, c'est moi* Churchill." He told them not to lose
> heart, that in due time, the free world would stir itself and
> relieve the French of their long night. "So," he said, "Sleep
> well, my Frenchmen, sleep well to gather strength for the
> morning, for the morning shall come."
> I sleep each night a little better, a little more confidently
> because Lyndon Johnson is my President. For I know he lives
> and thinks and works to make sure that for all Americans, and

indeed, the growing body of the free world, the morning shall always come. (p. 96)

Another top aide, George Reedy (1970), stressed far more conflictual traits:

> As a rule, his language was colorful, pointed, and what can most charitably be described as "earthy." His "humor" was based chiefly on the contents of toilet bowls and he was addicted to "pie-in-the-face" practical jokes. His favorite spectator sport was watching bovine copulation and he gloried in summoning fastidious males to his bathroom, where conference and excretion could be intermingled. His consumption of beverage alcohol was for purposes other than sacramental and in quantities that did not accord with St. Paul's "a little wine for thy stomach's sake." All of these activities would have offended his mother's Baptist instincts had she known about them, but they were all secondary to his ultimate apostasy — joining the Christian Church during a revival meeting. He claimed later that this was the outcome of a youthful love affair but it is impossible to avoid the suspicion that it was a gesture of rebellion. (p. 34)

Deeper in his book, Reedy comes to a somber assessment:

> In a very important sense, LBJ was a man who had been deprived of the normal joys of life. He knew how to struggle; he knew how to outfox political opponents; he knew how to make money; he knew how to swagger. But he did not know how to live. He had been programmed for business and for business only and outside of his programming, he was lost. (p. 74)

> Unfortunately for him, he believed the whole world was following the same path. He could not understand avocations, hobbies, or the loose form of banter which smooths so much of social discourse. When he misread the character of people of his own generation, it was usually because he found meanings in words that had no meaning other than social lubrication. He was totally devoid of small talk. Worse, he had no concept of the social usefulness of small talk. (p. 75)

Finally, rue sharpens to diatribe:

As a human being, he was a miserable person—a bully, sadist, lout, and egotist. He had no sense of loyalty (despite his protestations that it was the quality he valued above all others) and he enjoyed tormenting those who had done the most for him. He seemed to take a special delight in humiliating those who had cast in their lot with him. It may well be that this was the result of a form of self-loathing in which he concluded that there had to be something wrong with anyone who would associate with him.

Yet ambivalence prevails:

Nevertheless, he was capable of inspiring strong attachments even with people who knew him for what he was. Part of this was bemusement over the sheer size of his pettiness; part of it a mistaken belief that "he didn't mean for true more than half what he said." Even today, I can still feel a certain affection for him regardless of the agony of some of my memories. (p. 157)

Another aide, repeating many anecdotes found in other volumes, contributed this:

Johnson's thirst was for ideas, even as his Presidential years moved inevitably toward an end, and he was attracted to those with imagination and the boldness to innovate. He did not necessarily demand that the idea men be overly blessed with political judgment. He would be the check and balance in that regard. And though he might put the stamp of idiocy on someone's scheme, it did not necessarily mean he wanted no more ideas from that individual. A staffer who could not bounce back from temporary defeat had no business working for Johnson. But when anyone in government submitted too many suggestions of little merit, or talked too freely to the press about maneuvers "the Johnson Administration" was considering (whether Johnson knew about them or not), or ran too frequently with the wrong political crowd, woe unto that man insofar as retaining any influence with the President. The usual fate was to be consigned to limbo, to perform meaningless tasks or none at all, until some twist of fate or changed events might restore him to favor. Dismissal from government was exceedingly rare, although a downtrodden outcast might ultimately resign receiving a letter of acceptance from the President praising him for patriotic service. (Christian, 1970, p. 10)

It was part of the Johnson legend that he was a man who drove his employees mercilessly, abused them without cause or limitation, and cast them aside when he had wrung all he could from their shattered psyches. This was a careless interpretation, at best. I am confident that nearly every member of the Johnson staff thought himself overworked or abused at one time or another, but only a few allowed such sensitivities to get the better of them. (p. 15)

The well-known producer of educational television Bill Moyers (1986) described, from his days as chief of staff, Johnson's many warring selves:

He was many things: proud, sensitive, impulsive, flamboyant, sentimental, earthy, mean at times, bold, euphoric, insecure, magnanimous, the best dancer in the White House since Washington, but temperamental, melancholy, and strangely ill at ease, as well. He had an animal sense of weakness in other men, on whom he could inflict a hundred cuts.

Again, it is the self of "his best moments" who carries the day:

But character is something that presidents transcend with the consequence of policy on history. And those of us who worked for him were willing to forgive personal flaws, as he forgave ours, because in his best moments he had such a large and generous vision of America as a prosperous, caring just society. (p. 178)

Apart from those in his immediate staff, Johnson's speechwriters had special encounters with their chief that revealed their idealization of him. Mooney related the following anecdote about his wish not to leave his wife during her miscarriage:

In either case, what he said was, "Bird has had miscarriages and I wasn't around."

Unable to think of any reply to that, I said nothing.

"You won't go then, is that it?"

"Senator, I can't," I said desperately.

"Usually if a man is working for another man he tries to do what his employer wants him to do."

The threat was unmistakable.

"I know that," I said, "and I won't complain about any decision you make."

For the first time he turned his gaze away from me and looked down at the floor. When he spoke again it was in a disjointed mumble to the effect that he had talked with his wife and she was grateful for the help I had given her with the letters while he was in the hospital and if I felt I shouldn't go to Texas she was on my side. But he sure as hell couldn't understand my attitude.

As I remained silent he suddenly brightened. "I'll tell you what you can do," he said, his voice normal again.

A few months earlier I had suggested to Johnson that I would like to write a book about him, a short biography. Engrossed wholly in the work of the Senate at the time, his reaction had been decidedly negative. Now, he said, he had changed his mind. Since I was not going to Texas and there would not be much to do in the Washington office, I could spend the fall writing the book.

"What you do," he concluded, in command again, "you study that little campaign biography you wrote about Coke Stevenson in 1948 and then you write a book like that about me. Except," he added quickly, "better and longer. You didn't have as good a subject in Coke." (pp. 65–66)

Richard Goodwin (1988) expressed his unique experiences of Johnson in the following:

"I am not going to have anything more to do with the liberals. They won't have anything to do with me. They all just follow the communist line—liberals, intellectuals, communists. They're all the same. I detest the United Nations. They've tried to make a fool out of me. They oppose me. And I won't make any overtures to the Russians. They'll have to come to me. In Paris, Gargarin [Yuri Gargarin] (Soviet cosmonaut) refused to shake hands with the astronauts. I sent those astronauts myself, and what he did was a personal insult to me. I can't trust anybody anymore. I tell you what I'm going to do. I'm going to get rid of everybody who doesn't agree with my policies. I'll take a tough line — put Abe Fortas or Clark Clifford in the Bundy job. I'm not going in the liberal direction. There's no future with them. They're just out to get me, always have been."

I accompanied Moyers back to his office. "We were both shaken, alarmed," I noted in my diary, "not so much at the content of Johnson's statements — surely he didn't mean to halt all discussions with the Soviet Union or pull out of the United Nations — but at the disjointed, erratic flow of thought, unrelated events strung together, yet seemingly linked by some incomprehensible web of connections within Johnson's mind. He won't act on his words, but he believes they're true."

On June 28, I recorded in my diary that Johnson had "asked me and Bill if we thought Tom Wicker was out to destroy him, if Wicker was caught up in some sort of conspiracy against him. We said no, that he writes some favorable and some unfavorable stories, but we couldn't convince him. Then he suddenly switched the subject to say he thought Bobby Kennedy was behind the public assassination of Ed Clark — whom he had made ambassador to Australia. Without waiting for any reply, he went on to say that he had agreed to appoint Harlan Cleveland to the number-four job in the State Department but now he wouldn't appoint him dog catcher because he thought he leaked the story to Reston about the U.N. speech." (p. 401).

William White (1964), columnist and friend of Johnson, offered a "summary":

> . . . a child of the Great Depression, a partial creator and a full participant in the turn of this country away from the old, nearly total economic individualism toward the responsible social discipline which broke that depression and began the

long, still accelerating process of homogenization into a grayer but stronger American society....

> He is one of the most talented politicians in our history, alternately confident and skeptical, outgoing and reserved, tough and compassionate, born to action but sometimes electing to pause in long thought. Can such a man attain three enormously difficult goals: First, an end to political sectionalism in the United States; second, a final accommodation of a race issue that is the greatest domestic problem in a nation now insulated from the shocks of an economic disaster; and third, the beginning, at least, of a Western victory in the Cold War, or else a resolution of that war on terms more bearable for the free world? (p. 169)

Sam Houston Johnson (1969), brother, an attorney, and a politician, lived much of his life in service to his older brother. His book, *My Brother Lyndon*, records everything for which Johnson became famous in Washington—the driving energy, the toughness of his leadership, especially toward his staff, and the single-minded interest in his own needs and his concomitant lack of empathy. Sam Houston Johnson was among those who ordinarily suffered his brother's outbursts without protest:

> Yet, in spite of his readiness to understand the weaknesses and foibles of his Senate colleagues, Lyndon was a bit more demanding with members of his personal staff. They had to work long extra hours, often neglecting their home lives, and suffering the constant threat of "being fired" for some slight infraction. I put quotation marks around "being fired" because he didn't really fire people; that was just his way (admittedly unpleasant) of showing his displeasure with somebody's work. (p. 92)

> About the closest he's ever come to apologizing (at least to my personal knowledge) was an incident that occurred some years ago. He had asked me to bring home some documents he

needed for a trip he was making with President Truman, and I, in turn, asked my secretary to take them from the files and put them in my briefcase. Halfway home (I was giving her a lift to her apartment), she told me she had forgotten them. Not wanting me to drive back in the heavy traffic on that hot, muggy day, she offered to go for them in a taxi and bring them to me at a cocktail lounge nearby. While she was picking them up, Lyndon saw the file and grumbled about Sam Houston's forgetfulness. She told me about it when she handed me the documents. As things turned out, Lyndon got home just before I did, and he confronted me in the driveway.

"Goddammit, Sam," he said. "Why can't you do anything right? I told you to get those papers...." (p. 93)

I was still in my silent pout the next morning when we drove to work. Finally as we were speeding through Rock Creek Park, he turned and said, "About those papers yesterday, let's forget it, Sam Houston."

"Okay," I said, knowing that he was trying to apologize but was painfully unable to say, "I'm sorry." (p. 94)

Hubert Humphrey was a devoted—at times irrationally so—vice president to Johnson. Omitted from the usual coverage of his relationship with Johnson are all the occasions when Johnson vented the hostility to his second in command which he reserved for people he "owned." His abusiveness then became near-violent, especially over minor infractions, but also at attitudes that might or might not have existed. Humphrey was a loyal soldier to Johnson, whom he held in such high regard that he may be said to have pedestalized a man who demeaned him and ultimately caused his downfall in American politics. As Humphrey's biographer, Edgar Berman (1979) describes the relationship:

He had no idea of the depth of LBJ's quirks, his irrational secretiveness, and his suspicions of disloyalty.

Humphrey's initial trouble with LBJ was not caused by personality clashes, but by Humphrey's initiative in matters of substance—mainly Vietnam. It started a few weeks after the inauguration at a Cabinet luncheon when he opposed a bombing of North Vietnam. The paranoid Johnson took Hubert's opinion as an almost treasonous abandonment of the new Administration team's continuation of the Kennedy policy of strong reaction to aggression. Hubert's stand did him no dishonor—only grief—and alienated him from the White House as few other vice presidents had ever been. Johnson's belief that Humphrey was disloyal not only attested to LBJ's irrationality, but to his growing irascibility when it came to the war. He was not merely cold and distant; he began making certain nasty slurs against Humphrey that eventually got back to the vice president and tormented him.

For example, Johnson blamed Humphrey for almost every leak that ever came from the White House and would rant, "Hubert runs his mouth ninety miles an hour without thinking." (p. 92)

In the midst of the campaign, when Humphrey was trying to make inroads into Texas, Johnson had him down to the ranch (only once) with the strict proviso of "no press." A few days later, he had Nixon and Agnew down (both of whom he claimed to despise) with full press coverage and front-page pictures all over the country.

It was here that not only Humphrey's friends, but some of Johnson's said, "I told you so—break with the SOB." But even after that, I heard him say over and over again, "No, Governor; no, Mayor, I won't resign the vice presidency. I won't undercut the president just to make myself look good." (p. 94)

Foremost in the category of those who held Johnson in high regard, accepted him as their leader, or who existed in his clutches was none other than his wife, Lady Bird Johnson. Exorbitant as was the traditional role of helpmate in the Johnson's milieu and period, Lady Bird played it inerrantly. She became his secretary, hostess, sexual object, psychotherapist, valet, travel agent, nurse, champion, lodestar. In her chronicle of her various missions (*A White House Diary*, 1970), she reported days crammed with activities, all geared to performance as the perfect First Lady, always attempting to maintain her husband in equilibrium. When he sank into a depression, shortly before the 1964 Democratic convention, he became convinced he should not run for the presidency. Her letter to him helped him emerge from this temporary loss of self-worth:

> He did not believe he should accept the nomination. He did not want to go to Atlantic City. I do not remember hours I ever found harder.... At one point during the afternoon I went walking on the South grounds with Linda. We lay down under one of the big, spreading evergreens and talked and talked. Sometime during the afternoon, I went back inside and wrote Lyndon a letter:

> THE WHITE HOUSE
> WASHINGTON
> The President

> Personal

> Beloved—

> You are as brave a man as Harry Truman—or FDR—or Lincoln. You can go on to find some peace, some achievement amidst all the pain. You have been strong, patient, determined beyond any words of mine to express.

> I honor you for it. So does most of the country.

> To step out now would be wrong for your country, and I can see nothing but a lonely wasteland for your future. Your friends would be frozen in embarrassed silence and your enemies jeering.

> I am not afraid of Time or lies or losing money or defeat.

> In the final analysis I can't carry any of the burdens you talked of—so I know it's only your choice. But I know you are as brave as any of the thirty-five.

> I love you always
> Bird

The answer to my letter came on the night of August 27 when Lyndon stood before the Democratic National Convention and accepted the nomination of his party for President of the United States. (p. 192)

After Johnson's hospitalization for gallbladder surgery, she wrote in her usual vein of mixed idealization, concern, and subservience:

> By every barometer Lyndon seems to be progressing well. My chief fear is that he will return too soon to too much work. There are no rabbits in the hat; he is no superman. I know how much of his success is made up of 2 o'clock nights, of dogged determination, and of calling forth from himself and from everyone around him the last ounce of strength. I don't want him to begin that again on sheer nerve. In six weeks he can build up a backlog of strength. But everything was going so smoothly, I thought I could take off for two important destinations—the beauty parlor and the foot doctor. The first stop—the White House swimming pool for thirty quick laps, with Bess and Ashton walking up and down beside the pool, asking for decisions on engagements—all regretted—and on special correspondence and office problems. (*A White House Diary*, p. 328)

Thus, among the great range of people who came under the ever-increasing power of the one-time enterprising college student organizing a political campaign, now leader of the free world, there were those who became his subjects. To some of his followers, Johnson represented a godlike figure, to be followed unquestionably in whatever direction he took. Lady Bird Johnson, Sam Houston Johnson, George Christian, Jack Valenti, Walter Jenkins, and George Reedy were among those for whom Johnson had become their leader.

Others acknowledged his leadership; but out of their fear of his power to inflict pain—abandonment, criticism, shaming. Into this category fell Richard Goodwin, Bill Moyers, and Arthur Goldberg. There were others to whom Johnson had become a charismatic leader to be followed, quoted, and imitated: Merle Miller, Hubert Humphrey, and Hugh Sidey were all men who experienced LBJ as larger than life. His "unusual" behaviors on the floor of the Senate, in his washroom, in his bedroom—which will be described—were carefully observed to be published in newspapers, magazines, and books. Alfred Steinberg, Ronnie Dugger, and Merle Miller were among those writers who were caught up by this facet of Johnson either in direct exchanges with him or in scholarly investigation.

JOHNSON IN SEARCH OF SELF-STRUCTURE

To another group, Johnson's behavior was what is usually called sycophantic or fawning. In these relationships, which began early, Johnson was the perennial youngster imbued with overflowing admiration and awe for an idealized mentor. As will be later elaborated, these relationships derived from failed parental functions. They constitute the residue of parental deprivation of the specific needs of infants and children for self-nurturance.

Here we investigate the behavior that Johnson manifested in securing and maintaining the relationships in which he sought to gratify his archaic self-needs—the residue of his failed human encounters within his family. Next we will document a sample of significant relationships in Johnson's interpersonal history in which he opened to his human targets his well of appetites for relief of his self-tensions, his "mirroring" deficits, and his need for "calming."

One of the earliest targets away from the home scene from whom Johnson attempted to extract self-

affirmation was the local schoolteacher. Ms. Kate Die-
drich was a strapping six-foot adolescent who taught
the first seven grades in the school, half a mile east of
the Johnson farm near Stonewall, Texas. Lyndon could
cajole her into giving him special attention. She had to
place him on her lap in front of the assembled young-
sters, and only then would he read for her (Caro, 1981;
Rebekah Baines Johnson, 1965; Kearns, 1976; Steinberg,
1968).

During that same period, before the Johnson family
moved to Johnson City when Lyndon was five, he vis-
ited regularly with his paternal grandfather, Sam Ealy
Johnson, Sr. His grandfather was, as Johnson later recalled, "the perfect escape from all my problems at
home" (Kearns, 1976, p. 28).

> I sat, beside the rocker on the floor of the porch thinking
> all the while how lucky I was to have as a granddaddy this big
> man with the white beard who had lived the most exciting life
> imaginable. (Kearns, 1976, p. 28)

Grandfather had been a genuine cowboy and participated in the cattle drives eastward that had become legendary by the time Lyndon heard these enrapturing
stories.

In Johnson's passage through childhood and adolescence, he structured many relationships in which he
became the petitioner for the other's power. As we will
later describe more fully, his leader during those times
was his father, Sam Ealy Johnson, Jr. This dyad came to
a tragic end for Lyndon and his family when Sam Ealy
lost the family fortune through the failures of his cotton
enterprise.

It is essential to remember that Rebekah Baines
Johnson was always the matriarch to Lyndon, his sib-

lings, his father, and all in the community who knew her. During his childhood and adolescence, although his mother was an idealized figure, Johnson fought bitterly against her values. Ultimately he capitulated to her design for him, and entered the world of the educated classes. But this was not without a long struggle through childhood and adolescence in which he played the rebel—who drank, smoked, and womanized. It is a familiar Southern scenario, but with a certain desperate heightening.

As a young adult, Johnson enrolled at a local teacher's college, and became a different person from the construction worker he had been whose life was given to drinking, driving fast and dangerously, and tomcatting around (Kearns, 1976; Caro, 1980). Suddenly the road-running rakehell "became" the skinny, quick-moving high-energy student and socializer completely concentrated on "getting ahead." A major self-striving—till now an unformed and unrecognized feature of Johnson's self—came to fruition, the drive to obtain needed supplies of worth ("mirroring") and of the yearning to gain "direction" (in psychological terms, the need for the idealized parent imagoes).

At San Marcos College, Johnson became attached to two major figures: Dean Cecil Evans and Professor Harry Greene (Pool, Craddock, & Conrad, 1965). Johnson's wooing of these men and others, to follow on his path to power, fell into a ritual that soon became formalized. He would first offer flattery, adulation, and emulation of the admired object, to the point of gross identification. After his incorporation of the idol, Johnson would adopt the mentor's behavior now merged with his own self. He enacted the role of President Evans, swaggering through the halls of San Marcos. He became Professor Greene in language and gesture with other students, as if he was the debating coach. Demonstrating this process is an editorial that Johnson wrote, guaranteed to ensure President Evans' acceptance of Johnson:

> Great as an educator and as an executive, Dr. Evans is greatest as a man. Here we find a man who cherishes a fellowship with the humanities of life. He plans for deeds that live, leaving indelible impress on the lives of the youth of the college. With depth of human sympathy rarely surpassed, unfailing cheerfulness, geniality, kind firmness and friendly interest in the youth of the state, Dr. Evans has exerted a great influence for good upon the students of S.W.T.S.T.C. He finds great happiness in serving others. (Caro, 1983, p. 149)

When Robert Caro interviewed former students of San Marcos who remembered Johnson, they commented most frequently on his tactics in insinuating himself into a relationship with faculty members; and even more vehemently on his tactics in insinuating himself into leadership positions on the campus:

> When dealing with members of the administration and faculty in person, in fact, Johnson displayed an admiration so profound that fellow students say that if they described it fully, "no one would believe it." If, for example, a professor held an informal bull session on the "quadrangle" and Johnson was attending, he could be found sitting at the professor's feet. "Yes, literally sitting at his feet." A classmate says: if the professor was sitting on a bench, students might be standing around him, or sitting next to him, but one student, Lyndon Johnson, would often be sitting on the ground, his face turned up to the teacher, an expression of the deepest interest and respect on his face. "He would just drink up what they were saying, sit at their knees and drink it up, and they would pour out their hearts to him." (p. 150)

> The professor at whose feet Johnson sat most often was H. M. Greene, a history professor and debate coach; Johnson

may have received a "D" in the debate course taught by another professor, but he made Greene's debating team, much to
the surprise of students who, like one member of the team,
considered him "very forceful, but really not a good speaker at
all." (p. 151)

... his fellows would be astonished by his frantic, almost
desperate aggressiveness—that aggressiveness would have
been familiar to his college classmates. The desire to dominate,
the need to dominate, to bend others to his will—and the
manifestation of that need, the overbearingness with subordinates that was as striking as the obsequiousness with supe-
riors—had been evident at San Marcos. The tendency to
exaggeration—to untruthfulness, in fact—the sensitivity to
the slightest hint of criticism, the energy, the fierce, unquenchable drive that made him a man who worked harder than any
other men—his college classmates would have found those
qualities familiar, too. Other qualities of Lyndon Johnson less
immediately evident to others were present not only in Washington but at San Marcos: the viciousness and cruelty, the joy
in breaking backs and keeping them broken, the urge not just
to defeat but to destroy; the iron will that enabled him, once
his mind was set on a goal, to achieve it no matter what the
obstacles; above all, the ambition, the all-encompassing personal ambition that made issues impediments and scruples
superfluous. (p. 200)

From interviews, Caro found that Johnson's former
schoolmates at San Marcos—apart from a few who
remained friendly throughout college—disliked or
despised him. They remarked on his arrogance, his
propensity to exaggerate and lie, and his total self-
centeredness. The college publication, the *College Star*,
ran a humor column that awarded Johnson the degree of
M.B. (Master of Bullshit) (p. 160).

After Johnson left San Marcos, he taught high
school in Houston. At the beginning of his second year,
he received a surprise call from the newly elected member of Congress from the Fourteenth Congressional

District, Richard Kleberg, asking him to become his legislative secretary in Washington. Kleberg had been told of Lyndon Johnson by a young state senator, Welly Hopkins, whose campaign Johnson had worked in while still attending San Marcos College. He had originally attracted Senator Hopkins' attention when he gave an impromptu speech for a political patron of his father at a local political gathering in the summer of 1930. Hopkins sought Johnson out after the speech and offered him the job of managing his campaign for state senator. The following year he recommended Johnson's name to Kleberg for the post of congressional secretary. Kleberg was the heir to the legendary King ranch, and had recently won a special election to fill a vacancy in the Fourteenth Congressional District (Kearns, 1976).

When Johnson came to Washington as Kleberg's secretary, he came with his ambitions and his energy at full tilt. From the beginning, the staff at Kleberg's office were shocked by the twenty-two-year-old's energy. He opened the office before 8 A.M. and never left before 8 P.M. He dedicated himself to the work of running the office with no regard to his personal bodily or emotional needs.

Because the work involved obtaining favors for Kleberg's constituency, Johnson became knowledgeable about the different agencies in Washington and what they could offer Texans who were in need of political favors to procure federal contracts, arrange loans, and so on. In a remarkably short time he became known as the man to contact in Kleberg's office who really knew his way around Washington and how to make contact with various government agencies and commissions. One constituent who began to recognize Johnson as an important person in Washington was Alvin Wirtz, a powerful Texan attorney and former state senator who was to become another political father to Johnson in years to come.

Two other people who became major figures in Johnson's life also appeared at this time: Lady Bird Taylor and Sam Rayburn.

Lady Bird, the nickname for Claudia Alta Taylor of Karnack, Texas, was a shy, retiring girl whose mother had died when she was five. Her father, an old-time Southern patriarch, enlisted his sister-in-law to raise the little girl. Her Aunt Effie did little to infuse Lady Bird with vigor and self-worth. However, she did encourage and stimulate the child's interest in books.

Lady Bird first met Johnson in Austin when he was there on business for Kleberg in September 1934, and again when she was visiting a mutual acquaintance of hers and Johnson's, Eugenia Bahringer (Caro, 1983). Johnson managed to arrange a meeting with her and immediately "dived" at her with queries about her life, and monologues about his ambitions; and asked her to marry him (Steinberg, 1968, p. 82). From this moment, Johnson waged a campaign to convince Lady Bird of his need of her and his absolute devotion. She had apparently become an idealized figure, occupying a position akin to his experience of his mother.

As his biographer Doris Kearns (1976) noted, "To both mother and wife Lyndon Johnson would always ascribe a scarcely credible perfection" (p. 83). Of course as soon as she became a permanent part of his company, she also became an employee—laying out his clothes, filling the pens and the lighter he took with him, paying his bills, bringing him coffee in the morning and obeying his instructions about the amount of lipstick she wore, the length of her skirts, and her hairstyle.

Shortly after Johnson came to Washington, he sought out various people who had served with his father in the Texas legislature, including Wright Patman and Sam Rayburn, both now members of Congress. Another "political daddy" with whom Johnson established his particular brand of subservient bonding (idealization) was Maury Maverick (Steinberg, 1968).

Sam Rayburn, who came to the Congress in 1913 and had served with Sam Ealy Johnson in the Texas legislature, allowed young Johnson to talk to him from time to time when Johnson arrived in Washington in 1931. After Lady Bird became his wife, Johnson began inviting Mr. Sam, as everyone called him, to their apartment for dinner. Soon Rayburn began coming every Sunday morning and stayed for a good part of the day. He was then without family, a lifelong bachelor (except for a three-month early marriage).

As Hubert Humphrey said, "Their relationship was usually described as a father–son relationship" (Miller, 1980, p. 43). Rayburn became another "political daddy" to Johnson, teaching and encouraging him in the ways of the Congress, giving invaluable advice to the ever-admiring, eager-to-learn young man. In the same manner, Johnson sought out Congressman Wright Patman and then Congressman Maury Maverick; each became targets for this persistent seeker after knowledge. Each had a special store of political wisdom that Johnson eagerly drained (Caro, 1983; Kearns, 1976; Miller, 1980; Steinberg, 1968).

Two of Johnson's "political daddies," Rayburn and Maverick, were instrumental in rescuing Johnson when, in the summer of 1935, Dick Kleberg sacked him, allegedly because Congressman Kleberg's wife insisted that Johnson was using the Congressman's good offices for the advancement of his own career—which indeed he was. Johnson, who had begun sending letters to needy constituents from Kleberg's office, signed only by himself, was becoming known as the man in Washington to see if anyone from the Fourteenth District had a problem. When Kleberg's wife noted with alarm Johnson's domination of her husband's congressional office, she demanded that Johnson be fired (Steinberg, 1968, p. 93).

Rayburn and Maverick immediately went to work to urge President Roosevelt to appoint their young protégé to a significant new job, the Texas director of the new National Youth Administration, which was to be part of the $5 billion Works Progress Administration program. Maverick, himself a Roosevelt protégé, spoke directly to Roosevelt of his twenty-six-year-old friend. Rayburn, who never asked anyone for a favor, spoke to Senator Tom Connally, since he was certain the appointment would be considered a patronage issue. Roosevelt agreed, and appointed Johnson to the Texas-based position as director of the Texas NYA (Caro, 1983, p. 340; Steinberg, 1968, p. 94).

Now back home in Texas, Johnson went to work with a passion for the NYA. It was during this time that one of his "political daddies" from the past reemerged— Alvin Wirtz, whose law office was in the same building in Austin as the offices of the NYA. Johnson and his young colleagues, many of them old friends from San Marcos, were quite successful in making themselves of service to many young people using the NYA grants to keep them in school during the throes of the Great Depression.

In 1937, when Congressman James Buchanan suddenly died, Johnson's chance to become a congressman irrupted without warning. This event ushered in still another contact with Alvin Wirtz. Wirtz had counted on Buchanan to help him and the Brown and Root Construction Company in the remaining construction of a project important to them in Texas, the Marshall Ford Dam. Specifically, Buchanan was to draw up a bill in Congress which authorized the contract to build the dam, since the land on which the dam was being constructed was not owned by the federal government. Wirtz was eager for a replacement for Buchanan whom he could control.

When Johnson and Lady Bird came to him for advice about the empty congressional seat, Wirtz told Johnson to run for office; told them how much money was needed immediately ($10,000) for "seed money"; and provided Johnson with the campaign strategy to get elected: Back FDR to the hilt, especially in his plan to enlarge the U.S. Supreme Court with his appointees—the "court-packing" plan (Caro, 1983; Dugger, 1982; Steinberg, 1968). Wirtz was to function for Johnson as a major fund-raiser, especially with the oil and construction interests. He also lined up support from such people as Charles Marsh, the publisher of several Texas newspapers, especially the dailies, the *Austin American* and the *Austin Statesman*.

Alvin Wirtz, Johnson called "my dearest friend, my most trusted counselor. From him...I gained a glimpse of what greatness there is in the human race" (Caro, 1983, p. 373). Lady Bird called him the "lodestar of our lives." His picture hangs prominently at the Johnson ranch with Lady Bird's inscription: "Senator A.J. Wirtz— The Captain of My Ship, Any Day" (Caro, 1983, p. 373). And so Johnson won his first political campaign and became the member of Congress from the Tenth Congressional District of Texas in 1937 by 3,000 votes over his nearest opponent (Caro, 1983, p. 436).

The next fish that Johnson snared in his net woven of kowtowing was the biggest catch of them all, the boss, Franklin Delano Roosevelt, the savior of the Great Depression. In what had now became the typical Johnson treatment for evoking positive responses from older men with power—the remarkable set of interpersonal skills to cull favor which he had polished since his early days—he set out to net the king fish, President Roosevelt. First, he petitioned his reporter friends in the Associated Press and elsewhere to flash across the country the "good news" that a Texas supporter of the Roosevelt party line, especially the court-packing scheme, had won. The *Washington Post* headline on April 10, 1936, read "Texas Supporter of Court Changes Appears Elected." Then he asked local fans to send wires to Franklin Roosevelt in the White House announcing Johnson's victory as a manifestation of his support of Roosevelt.

A stroke of luck was providential at this moment. Roosevelt was planning a fishing trip in the Gulf of Mexico and would wind it up in Galveston. Johnson saw his chance to meet there with FDR. He entreated the governor of Texas to arrange a meeting. Not only did the meeting take place but Roosevelt, succumbing to the Johnson treatment, arranged for him to ride on the train with him all the way to Fort Worth, 200 miles away.

After that one-day trip, Johnson's future in Washington was in no small way assured. Robert Caro (1983), after interviewing Thomas Corcoran, a key Roosevelt aide and New Deal strategist, wrote of Roosevelt: "He said, 'I've just met the most remarkable young man. Now I like this boy, and you're going to help him with anything you can'" (p. 448).

As Caro went on to relate, Roosevelt himself helped Johnson with both hands. He arranged for Johnson to become a member—unheard-of for a freshman Congressman—of the Naval Affairs Committee. He (Roosevelt) talked to Harold Ickes and Harry Hopkins about the "remarkable young man" from Texas and told them to give him a leg up.

Corcoran, along with Ben Cohen, another major strategist of the New Deal, befriended Johnson and helped him cultivate people whom he used during his entire political career: James Rowe, Abe Fortas, Tex Goldschmidt, and William O. Douglas. All were key figures as theoreticians and strategists, not as field marshals, but as lieutenants in the New Deal. Johnson threw himself energetically into this group, which became a vehicle for learning, gossip, recommendations for passing appointments around and, for a while, the major social outlet for himself and Lady Bird. They all admired Johnson for what, as Abe Fortas proclaimed: "The guy's got extra glands" (Caro, 1983, p. 456).

And so Johnson, as the years of his congressional tenure continued, became Roosevelt's man even above his loyalty to Rayburn. In fact, as Evans and Novak (1968) documented, his allegiances to these two "political daddies" at times made for competition between them. Once Roosevelt used Johnson to quash a resolution by the Texas congressional delegation which included Rayburn's rebuking the famed labor leader John L. Lewis, who had labeled the vice president from Texas a "poker-playing, whiskey-drinking, evil old man" (p. 11).

In 1940, when Vice President Garner attempted a stop-Roosevelt movement at the Chicago Democratic convention, Roosevelt, through Johnson and the new

Under Secretary of the Interior, Alvin Wirtz (an appointment that had been made through Johnson's intervention), exerted pressure on the Texas delegation — which
of course included Rayburn — to issue a statement
pledging their loyalty to Roosevelt. These actions on
Johnson's part were responsible for the cooling of the
Rayburn–Johnson relationship and the warming of the
Roosevelt–Johnson connection.

When Congressman Johnson obtained the necessary authorization for the Brown and Root Construction
Company to complete their work on the Marshall Ford
Dam, he gained the friendship of another man destined
to be yet another older man who would be important in
his future. Herman Brown was to be one of Johnson's
major financial contributors in his bids for the Senate, as
well as making substantial financial outlays for his bids
for Congress in 1938 (Caro, 1983; Dugger, 1982).

In these same years, Johnson found yet another par-
entlike figure from whom he could derive power. This
was the previously mentioned Charles E. Marsh, pub-
lisher of the *Austin American Statesman* and other influential newspapers throughout Texas. He was also
involved in real estate, oil wells, tracts of land, and used
his wealth to play patron to a host of sycophantic young
men, including Lyndon Johnson.

Johnson identified Marsh early as a target for his
needs to use the power of the Texas press which Marsh
controlled, as well as make use of Marsh's wealth for
contributions to his political campaigns. And so Johnson began his "treatment" of Charles Marsh, which included frequent trips to the Marsh mansion in Virginia,
"Longlea," with and without Lady Bird (Caro, 1983;
Steinberg, 1968).

Here the congressman in 1937 met Marsh's mistress, Alice Glass, then a glamorous twenty-six years old to Marsh's fifty, who soon completely captivated Johnson. According to Robert Caro (1983), Alice told her cousin and her sister that she and Johnson became lovers in 1938, using Marsh's own apartments in the Mayflower Hotel and in the Allies Inn for their liaisons. Alice Glass, although three years younger, became Johnson's social and cultural mentor. She helped him to dress, improved his table manners, read him poetry, and softened his image (Caro, 1983, p. 483).

When Johnson, on his second try, became a senator, he entered into association with the last of his "political daddies," Richard Russell of Georgia. After his apprenticeship with Russell, his political self could be said to be complete, a synthesis of the political skills of many. Once in the Senate, Johnson knew—as he always knew in these situations—that he had to get to the seat of power in order to gain the control that offered the vital elixir his self craved. In the Senate, it was the Senator from Georgia, Richard Russell, who was the undisputed boss of the inner circle, the man to whom every member turned for direction. It was also Russell who commanded the conservative bloc of senators who could get legislation passed or rejected through filibusters.

Once again, Johnson made an accurate diagnosis of the essential qualities of the self to whom he was to attach. This time it was not a hyperassertive Herman Brown, a mirror-hungry Charles Marsh, or an affection-starved Sam Rayburn. It was a dignified, almost monastic lifelong bachelor. Again the chameleonlike Johnson took it on himself to emulate another persona in manners, dress, social and intellectual interests, and philosophy. It was no accident that his maiden speech as a senator was to advocate the continuance of the filibuster rule, which Russell called "one of the ablest I have ever heard" (Kearns, 1976, p. 105). Johnson became a Southern conservative overnight, even though he had never been exposed to the indoctrination necessary to engender the conviction that separation of the races was a necessary condition for life in the United States. Indeed, having been raised in a town where there were no blacks, Johnson had never absorbed this indoctrination.

Johnson toned down his effusiveness, walked slower, dressed more conservatively, and always called Russell "Senator." He made sure Russell noted his hardworking qualities and insinuated himself into his life by "being around" at night so that Russell would see him (Kearns, p. 105). He invited Russell, the bachelor, to his home for Sunday brunch and to read the papers. The carefully nurtured contact paid off as Russell, responding to the ever-eager Johnson, began to regard him as a worthy student of his knowledge and skills. Continuing his campaign, Johnson contrived to secure a place on the Armed Service Committee so that Russell now saw even more of his assiduous student. But the real payoff came some four years later when Johnson once again seized an opportunity for advancement and placed his name for consideration as the minority leader of the Senate with Russell's blessings. The next milestone, in 1955, was the post of majority leader—and fame.

In the view of most political critics of the 1950s, Johnson was an extraordinarily competent majority leader of the Senate. He surpassed all others in developing an organization free of divisiveness and rendering almost total loyalty to Johnson's commands. There were complaints from senators and others about his secrecy; his insistence on limiting debate, and that the executive branch initiate most policies, including those on foreign affairs. But on the whole, most senators rallied behind his firm leadership.

One aspect of his majority leader self that was conspicuous was a seeming absence of ideals to guide his actions. His need to triumph, his fear of defeat and loss of control over "his" Senate—these were the important motives; never his *values* as the unswerving element in negotiation to serve passage of a bill. In 1957, he championed the highly controversial civil liberties legislation by mitigating the fears of the South—he promised to obliterate the specter of invading federal troops and reassured the North that the bill could pass if its provocative aspect, such as Title III, was eliminated. In one part of the Senate cloakroom, he whispered to a Southerner that the worst of "the nigger bill" was coming up; in another part, he would urge a Northern liberal to get ready for debate so that "we can make sure this long-overdue bill for the benefit of Negro-Americans would pass" (Kearns, 1976, pp. 149–150).

As he scored ongoing triumphs as the Senate majority leader, Johnson now discarded his most recent mentor in a fashion reminiscent of his termination of the relationship with "Mister" Sam Rayburn. Once again his ambitions far outweighed his loyalty to his current mentor, and once again the relationship ended without the interiorization of the mentor's values. Johnson suddenly was no longer the reactionary Southerner he had been while under Russell's tutelage. He was again exposed as the quintessential political operator, using whatever—including a Southern drawl and a temporary affiliation with the reactionary viewpoint—to make his way upward in the slippery world of politics.

In the relationships which have been described and documented, Johnson, utilizing a variety of interpersonal tactics, was able to structure these connections so as to draw the self supplies necessary to fuel his pervasively depleted self. Of course, these encounters offered little of lasting benefit to sustain Johnson's ever-flagging self-worth. He was destined to the end of his days to be on the make for new opportunities to infuse his self with exogenous sources of approval and calming.

JOHNSON'S COMRADES

Another group significant to Johnson was a small cadre of men who served as advisers and comrades and in whose presence Johnson was uplifted, or given guidance. They were what psychoanalytic self psychologists call "mature" selfobjects. This phrase refers to those figures who function as transient caretakers, whose interest and attention evoke remembrances of "archaic" selfobjects—the parental caretakers of one's past.

The terms advisers and comrades used above are to be taken in a special sense in reference to Johnson, since, as we have seen, his capacity to enter into the bond of friendship was limited to the needs he had of the relationship. He could and did turn from the ideologies and needs of Rayburn, Roosevelt, Russell, and many others dating from his early days. Among these so-called comrades, two will be singled out: Abe Fortas and Dean Rusk; although other colleagueships could be described from childhood and adolescence (for example, the Crider brothers), from the San Marcos period (Boody Johnson), from the early Washington days (Bill Payne), as Congressman (Jim Rowe), and in the Senate (Bob Kerr). These relationships were not genuinely egalitarian. Johnson invited or permitted advice or direction in a limited way with these men, and he might transiently unfold himself for the psychological functions of direction and approval which these "comrades" gave. But he always retained the leadership in each of these relationships and, as always, he never gave himself over entirely.

Abe Fortas became an ally and friend of Johnson's when Fortas was a rising star in Harold Ickes' Department of the Interior. They had some roots in common — Fortas from the poor Jewish district of Memphis, Johnson from the poor hill country of Texas. Johnson became quickly aware of the legal genius of Fortas, as well as of the traits that Johnson admired most in men — pragmatism and the ability to get the job done. Fortas was enlisted early by Johnson, Wirtz, and Brown to save the Marshall Ford Dam in Johnson's district, which was in danger of losing its financing. Fortas succeeded in finding a legal remedy to solve the financial distress of the Brown's Construction schemes, and save the dam (Murphy, 1988). From then on Johnson and his cohorts sought him out for legal advice, business schemes and later on, as Johnson advanced in power, to become an advice-giver on a variety of matters, from writing State-of-the-Union addresses to giving counsel on Vietnam foreign affairs.

Fortas' leadership in the matter of Johnson's disputed "victory" in the 1948 senatorial race undoubtedly saved Johnson's political career (Murphy, 1988). Fortas became one of Johnson's most important confidants after the death of Alvin Wirtz in 1951 (Murphy, 1988). Thereafter, he was known as the "court of last resort" to Johnson. Johnson wrote him when he was senator:

> I am deeply grateful for your friendship and believe me
> there have been many times in the past months when I would
> have been helpless had I not had the privilege of tapping your
> rich store of wisdom. (Murphy, 1988, p. 104)

Even though the two men had different interests
and styles—Fortas the cool unflappable one, Johnson
always in motion; Fortas the gifted amateur violinist
who collected antiques, Johnson who ate with his
hands—they had a common love of power and a common disdain for philosophy and ideology. And Fortas,
for his part, valued highly his role as consultant to the
senator, then the vice president, and then the president.

Johnson, he said, had a "pack rat" mind; it was a
great instrument (Murphy, 1988, p. 124). Fortas was referring to the remarkable facility of Johnson's in storing
all manners of information to be retrieved and utilized
at an appropriate time. By the time Johnson came to the
White House, it was well known that Abe Fortas and
another well-known Washington attorney and advice-
giver, Clark Clifford, the "Bobbsey Twins" (Christian,
1970, p. 107), were the "court of last resort" for Johnson
when he had a decision to make, and his advisors were
giving him conflicting opinions (Murphy, 1988, p. 125).

As the Vietnam war began to be a losing proposition,
Fortas became the president's most trusted confidant.
Whether it was over a halt in bombing or discussion of
negotiations with the enemy, Johnson's most trusted
ally was Fortas, although Fortas, now a Justice of the
Supreme Court, was going against the established tradi-
tion of keeping the distance between the executive
branch and the judicial.

President Johnson's relationship with his Secretary
of State Dean Rusk also had elements of genuine friend-

ship. Both men were Southerners, both had risen from hard times. On the surface, they were remarkably unalike. Johnson was of course volcanic, earthy, crude. Rusk was sphinxlike, always contained, imperturbable, always stressing intellectual and emotional mastery. However, Johnson always appreciated Rusk's devotion to him and to the country and counted on his honesty. He told Sam Houston Johnson (1969): "He's a damned good man. Hardworking, bright, and loyal as a beagle" (p. 117). President Johnson was relatively inexperienced in foreign policy; but Rusk bolstered his confidence, reminding Johnson that as vice president he had traveled widely and kept in touch with major foreign policy issues.

Rusk and Johnson were certainly good allies. They supported each other's positions and, even in the complex worlds of the American president and his secretary of state, were friendly, and had admiration for each other.

DISCUSSION: THE MANY SELVES OF LYNDON JOHNSON—AN EMPATHIC DIAGNOSIS

One of Johnson's presidential aides, Tom Johnson, put in a nutshell the focus of this volume in general and this chapter in specific:

> All of the people who came in contact with Johnson—his family, his friends, his political associates, the members of the White House staff—each of them had his or her slice of Lyndon Johnson. Now some of the slices are larger than others. Bill Moyers' slice is a very large slice. Mrs. Johnson's slice is surely the largest.
> But nobody has ever put all of the slices together. The

things that have been written about him, all of them are very
limited, taking in a very small slice. What has to be done is to
put all of the slices of the pie together. If it can be done. (Tom
Johnson quoted in Miller, 1980, p. xix)

The basis for our discussion of the Johnson self is
the data that we have described as, first, his self experiences in relating to those in his life to whom he was a
leader—his aides, Valenti, Christian; his wife, Lady
Bird; his protégés, Humphrey, Moyers. Secondly, it is
his experiences in relating to figures whom he put on a
pedestal, albeit always within a certain framework of
time and need—Dean Evans, Wirtz, Rayburn, FDR,
Richard Russell. Finally, it is his relating to those with
whom he had a relationship of neutrality and shared
needs—Fortas and Rusk.

THE SELFOBJECT/SELF ENCOUNTERS OF
LYNDON JOHNSON

The Imperious Self of Lyndon Johnson

Lyndon Johnson was a larger-than-life character for
a great number of people from his earliest days. He
always demanded center stage, from insisting on riding
the communal donkey to elementary school, to being
the best marble shooter in his neighborhood, to garnering all the academic and political honors in college, to
dropping in on the Pope with a statue of himself when
he was vice president. In all these grandiose behaviors,
Johnson demonstrated an imperative need to be the important person in any dyad, or in any room. When center stage was denied him, or there was a threat to his

being onstage at all, Johnson either fled, or became withdrawn or depressed.

A variant of this reaction to the threat of being removed from being in charge was his reaction to being criticized (including his being unable to say, "I'm sorry"). Johnson could never admit wrongdoing or wrong thinking, and no one ever heard him admit guilt over anything. If a reporter or TV commentator criticized or called attention to a defect in a policy of Johnson's, he would expect a call from Johnson that night, lambasting him for disloyalty to the flag and the country because they had attacked a sitting President of the United States.

Johnson's uneasiness about being criticized led to isolation and the need for secrecy. The acquisition of power was the panacea for all of Johnson's concerns over his inferiority. When Johnson did assume a leadership role, there were frequent episodes of "overkill." Johnson in command was often Johnson with a smoking gun. He had to snuff out any scintilla of weakness in his surround, or rebelliousness or criticism.

At times his need to maintain leadership resembled a caricature of the leader; he checked and rechecked work of his aides (and spied on their work at night). He was constantly anxious about secrecy and about people leaving him or usurping his power.

The clue to understanding this self-posture lies in the Johnson version of himself as the absolute monarch, or the exalted one brooking no controversy, and forcing all around him to become subjugated to his command, including following him to the bathroom in the White House to witness his bowel movements. Aides had to "snap to," just as Lady Bird Johnson had to, from the beginning of their marriage, and as Sam Houston Johnson had to, from their boyhood days as siblings. To buttress his ever-present concern about any display of weakness, he often practiced malevolence on whoever was in his field of vision—brother, wife, aides, or clerical help. They became the objects of a stream of abuse for any infraction, and if Johnson was wrong about who committed the error, they would receive no apology. The more frightened he became, the more intolerance he displayed.

All these data point to Johnson's leadership as having been marred by a fear of disclosure of defect or inferiority. His grandiosity was a compensation for his overwhelming fear of disclosure of a self of narcissistic (self-worth) deficit.

To those who followed him, the self they observed and followed was a leader who filled their needs for the imperial leader they found in Johnson. An affinity for an absolute monarch who exhibits the need for total control of his surround is perhaps not an attractive appetite, and may be difficult for some to empathize with. But surely, Johnson fulfilled selfobject needs for many of his followers.

If those who only knew this self described Johnson, they would highlight his episodes of lack of empathy and tantrums followed by instances of overgenerosity. They would count instances of his sadistic behavior, of his fear of disclosure (e.g., reporting a grossly inaccurate number of deaths of the military forces in Vietnam); of his fear and sadness when things were not going well, and, of course, of his emptiness and loneliness—the inability to unfold his intense fears of failure. No one shared with Johnson this inner self of ineptitude; this self was *never* on display.

THE SELF SEEKING ITS SELFOBJECT

For much of his life Johnson was hustling to effect a bond for the relief of his tension of *aloneness*. This is the central experience of those who have not become sufficiently infused with the psychic fuel of approval from archaic selfobjects in infancy.

Johnson was constantly extracting from his human or nonhuman environment whatever he could in the way of mirroring. He hit the ground running each day of his life; his wife never recalls him oversleeping. From his earliest childhood, his mother recalled that he would so often be running away from home that she unwittingly supplied him with the need gratification of enrolling him at school when he was only four years old.

Many of his self/selfobject efforts to obtain "mirroring" involved self transformations; posturing himself to obtain the vital-infusion of mirroring as we have documented. With women, he might tell them they resembled his mother (Christian, 1970). To Rayburn, he would become as if he was like his overcontrolled mentor. To FDR, he *was* at least temporarily ideologically bonded to the New Deal. To Russell, he was a committed anti-progressive Southerner. To his mother, and to Alice Glass, and, for a while, to Lady Bird, he was ever-ready to receive their ministrations.

But deserting the current selfobject for another, more gratifying one, or one more needed, was always his agenda. He turned away from Rayburn over the candidacy of Vice President Garner when FDR beckoned him. He did turn his back on the policies of FDR as soon as Roosevelt died, and it was expedient to become known as a senator with whom the oil interests could do business (Caro, 1983; Dugger, 1982).

Another facet of Johnson's quest for supplies from his surround was his need for garnering leadership strength. This is the infusion of calming and direction one obtains from the caretaker who originally picks up the infant and soothes him, and later in life directs and guides. Fusing with this idealized parent selfobject transmits the *calm* to one's self, and ordinarily contributes to the self the stability of firmly held ideals.

Thus, Johnson was not only mirror hungry, he was hungry for *calming*, for a stabilizing set of values with which he could identify; in short, hungry for an idealized leader whom he could follow, even if he would—as he always did—ultimately discard him or her, revealing his need, and his unfortunate defense against the need.

Johnson had countless "political daddies" and "idealized moms" with whom he attempted to fill this particular appetite for calming, soothing, direction, guidance, and values. From earliest boyhood attempting to emulate his father's swagger and vocal nuances, he created quite a stir in Johnson City (Caro, 1983; Kearns, 1976). At San Marcos he "became" Dean Evans and Professor Greene (Pool, Craddock, & Conrad, 1965). In his apprenticeship in Washington, he began to imitate the lobbyist Roy Miller (Miller, 1980) and to "listen" to the advice of Senator Alvin Wirtz (Caro, 1983). He even looked like Senator Richard Russell when he was insinuating himself into Russell's self—walking, talking, clothing himself in the Russell manner.

In each of these unconscious attempts to derive the needed self-structure from these selfobjects, Johnson ultimately failed. The reason was that he could not settle and "become" Russell's or FDR's or Rayburn's protégé over *time*. He could merge in some part, but never with the more complete unfolding of the self. He could not internalize the needed *structure,* in order to experience the needed calmness or direction. What he did derive from these idealized figures was a temporary identification. But his identifications were revealed to be pseudo-identifications, "as-if" phenomena (*as if* he was a liberal, or a Southerner, or had *any* genuine ideological facet of his value system). And once again we witness Johnson's flirtation with merging with the ideals of his selfobject leader in conflict with an inhibition—a fear—against becoming permanently bonded with the leader and his ideals. We surmise that the inhibition against merger was a resultant of the revived memory in Johnson of the wish to bond, coming into conflict with fearful or disappointing memories of leaders in his childhood, which will be discussed later in this book.

If observers of Johnson saw only this self seeking for its selfobject mirror, or idealized parent, they would only see a driven person in determined pursuit of a leader; sometimes overtly sycophantic, sometimes covertly sycophantic or restrained; but always, endlessly, *pursuing.*

THE JOHNSON SELF OF TWINSHIP

The final interpersonal encounters described in this chapter are of Johnson with Fortas and with Rusk, who are examples of those he sought out for peerlike relationships, for advice, counsel, debate, common political interests, and the like. These relationships were not archaic self/selfobject encounters, where Johnson "pedestalized" the men or their teaching. Fortas greatly admired Johnson, and Johnson greatly admired Fortas and Rusk and others; but not to the point of his usual sycophantic entreaties and obeisances. Fortas was perhaps the man most trusted of all of Johnson's associates; he was not experienced in any greater-than-life fashion. All these brother figures, greatly appreciated by Johnson, could be and were discarded when it suited him.

SUMMARY REMARKS

To understand the psyche of Lyndon Johnson, the observer must be mindful of the various selves which Johnson displayed with various people. What was Johnson attempting to derive from the particular person he was contacting? What fear or inferiority was he attempting to quell by the grandiose self he was revealing at another moment? Our task is now to put the data together in a case-study sequence in order to answer the question. *What* was the central experience of Lyndon Johnson in his major interactions in life, his aspirations, his fears, and his tactics?

Johnson's revealed and essential self was that of a man in a perpetual state of unrest, constantly *on* center stage, or *striving* for center stage. Whether he was grabbing at the lapels of his target, his mouth almost into the mouth of his victim, or sitting at the feet of his selfobject, Johnson himself was never to be forgotten. What ties together all the so-called "slices" of Johnson is the essential experiences of a man *never* able to achieve a sense of well-being. He was aware only that he had daily missions to perform which, if they did not succeed, would let down the floodgates to a massive loss of self-worth. Life consisted of *missions* and of people to *support the missions,* or who would give him the job of leading a mission and should the mission fail (as in the loss of an election, military failures in Vietnam, or the loss of a debating contest in Houston), he would reveal the self of enfeeblement.

Another set of findings which the psychohistorian and clinician must recognize are the talents and attributes of the subject under scrutiny. A related set of data are those of the revealed self-deficiencies of the scrutinized subject. And finally, the data of the subject's nonverbal behaviors and other attributes are important components. Johnson's appearance was striking; he was six foot-three, with a 220-pound frame. He often used his physical stature as an instrument for persuasion, intimidation, or sexual seduction. His prodigious memory, the "pack rat mind," as Fortas labeled it, was a source of wonder, as was his capacity to comprehend difficult legal arguments; he had a first-class mind. Another of his attributes in his adult life was discipline. He never came to a meeting without the necessary preparation and he never overslept.

On the negative side, a major finding of Johnson's self was his limitations as an empathizer. His capacity to introspect vicariously, to put himself in someone else's shoes, was quite limited. This latter observation is a cardinal finding of Johnson's self. From childhood to commander in chief of the armed services, Johnson did *not* experience the other's mortification or pain. He could and did inflict narcissistic wounds on others from which he did not recoil or experience remorse. This difficulty in self-functioning of Johnson's mature self we will call to attention again as we describe his operations in the Vietnam war and elsewhere.

The next chapter will describe the Johnson of observers "from the outside," so to speak. These observers were journalists and reporters and historians including David Halberstam, Merle Miller, Doris Kearns, Rowland Evans and Robert Novak, Robert Caro, Alfred Steinberg, and others.

Chapter 3

OBSERVERS FROM A DISTANCE

THE VIEW OF JOHNSON FROM JOURNALISTS, POLITICAL COMMENTATORS, AND HISTORIANS

This chapter will offer an overview of the Johnson story from a group of historians, journalists, and political commentators who have studied and written on the evolution of Johnson to the politician he became, on his presidency, on his downfall in the Vietnam era, and other aspects of the Johnson saga. Although some of these writers had been with Johnson in various relationships, during formal interviews, or in intimate discussions, or attended and participated at press conferences, they were all "observers at a distance." That is, their lives had not been affected by contact with Johnson as relatives, friends, and comrades and employees; nor was *his* life markedly affected by contact with these observers.

They therefore offer a unique historical version of

Johnson. Their observations reflect, of course, their level of psychological and sociological sophistication, their intent in writing about Johnson, their biases, and their personal feelings toward him, whether negative, warm, or friendly. Our goal is not simply to catalog their views, but to use their reaction to Johnson to characterize the public persona which Johnson displayed. It was this persona that people knew and voted for, and around which they rallied their positions for and against him.

The observers we have chosen to represent the body of Johnson literature range from academic historians to working journalists, the better, we hope, to provide an overview. We begin with the so-called investigative journalists such as Robert Caro, Doris Kearns, Alfred Steinberg, David Halberstam, Ronnie Dugger, and R. Evans and R. Novak. We will offer examples of the writings of the working journalists who wrote subjectively, such as William White, and dispassionately, as did Tom Wicker, Hugh Sidey, and Frank Cormier. We will also include the perspectives given by historical authors such as Paul Johnson.

THE INVESTIGATIVE JOURNALISTS

These writers either pursued the life story of Johnson in its entirety or concentrated on specific periods in Johnson's life story. They each attempted to go beyond the official memoirs of the Johnson story to arrive at an accurate rendering of the environmental influences on Johnson in childhood, in high school, and in college.

Robert Caro, a masterful investigator, pursued people throughout the continent to arrive at a valid appreciation of the forces that influenced Johnson and to obtain a version of Johnson throughout his development. His book, *The Years of Lyndon Johnson* (1983), offers a comprehensive account of the young Johnson through the eyes of his elementary school playmates, and his acquaintances in high school, in college, and later. The Johnson that Caro paints is a young boy, then a grown man (up to his days in the Senate), who from the day he began to walk was driven to be someone's center stage, attempting to capture someone's attention (later on, to capture votes, money, and power). This book is impressive in its assemblage of the details of Johnson's life. The reader is enabled to capture the image of the preteen Johnson swaggering around Johnson City giving recitations of the day's newspaper headlines. The reader can "see" the adolescent rebel, and the pushy college kid insinuating himself into the good graces of the president.

However, the reader is ultimately left without any appreciation of what intrapsychic pressures were fueling Johnson's persistent strivings to obtain narcissistic (self-worth) supplies. Piled on in massive detail are the data of the Johnson bullying and intimidating tactics, and his euphoria when he was victorious, but little interpretation toward an understanding of this complex man.

Caro's contribution to the Johnson literature is voluminous and offers invaluable data about Johnson's *behaviors*—what he had done and seen—without any recognition that the behavior derived from *in*trapsychic conflicts and deficits. Without the intrapsychic lens, the behaviors that Caro reports can only be viewed as an unusual degree of self-centeredness (Caro, 1983).

Doris Kearns' contribution to the Johnson myth is

unique, since she spent two years at the LBJ ranch after Johnson's departure from the presidency. He had sought her out to put together the presidential library and to work on his memoirs. Her biography, *Lyndon Johnson and the American Dream* (1976), is based on many interviews, including many early morning free-association sessions, laced with inconsistencies, exaggerations, and attempts by Johnson to evoke positive mirroring responses from the author. [For example, he told her she reminded him of his mother, a comment he often made, according to George Reedy (1970), to other women.] While Kearns' view of Johnson is clearly sympathetic, he gave her an insight into his experiences that was unique.

Kearns' book emphasizes the complexity of Johnson's relationship with his mother: Rebekah Baines Johnson was selective in her love. She doled it out as payment for acceding to her cultural and intellectual standards. Kearns recounts the paradoxes of Johnson's development: Manifestly he praised and revered his mother, in action he went against every one of her principles—he drank, womanized, was hostile to culture, and to people of culture.

Johnson's relationship with his father was also complex and ultimately disappointing. Johnson told Kearns his father was competitive and depreciating and unresponsive to Lyndon's yearning for his leadership. While Lyndon swaggered like him, spoke and told stories like him, and otherwise imitated his father, he was unable to internalize Sam Ealy's values into his self. The elder Johnson was honest to a fault, he was a totally committed populist; and he compromised with none in his long tenure as a state legislator. All these values never became LBJ's values; he compromised, he had very few principles to guide him, he could and did lie when he felt it was useful.

Kearns also was told of the raging conflict between Sam Ealy's rowdiness and alcoholism and Rebekah Baines's straitlaced attitude, so often colliding in the Johnson home in near-violent argument. Although she documented Johnson's fear of being passive, she failed to note that Johnson emerged from childhood with clear-cut symptoms of deprivation—not indulgence—of the child's needs for mirroring and calming-soothing direction. Johnson remained a person perpetually needy of the parental ministrations of mirroring (applause, admiration) and of the balm of comforting which comes from the calming-soothing parent.

Kearns understood that Johnson feared *confrontation*—he was always seeking consensus, or persuading his adversaries to come around to seeing things his way. She saw and described well that Johnson's unique qualities as Senate leader—primarily in reaching compromise, avoidance of conflict, and secrecy—were in opposition to the qualities required of a world leader. While Kearns does remind us that before each of his three elections (1948, 1964, 1968), he threatened withdrawal from the elections, and before almost every other election (1937, 1941, 1966), he became ill and required hospitalization, she did not collate her valuable findings to hypothesize that Johnson's behavior as a politician was fueled by lifelong self-needs and lifelong fears of unfolding these needs which so dominated his life (Kearns, 1976).

David Halberstam's study of Johnson (1972) begins:

> He was the elemental man, a man of endless restless ambition. Nothing was ever completed, each accomplishment was a challenge to reach for more. He was a politician the like

of which we shall not see again in this country, a man who
bridged very different Americas, his early days and attitudes
forged by earthy frontier attitudes and whose final acts as
President took us to the edge of the moon. He was a man of
stunning force, drive and intelligence and of equally stunning
insecurity. The enormity of his accomplishments never dimmed
the hidden fears which had propelled him in the first place; he
was in that sense, the most human of politicians. (p. 522)

Halberstam's account of Johnson in the presidency
and during the Vietnam war is filled with lucid observations of Johnson's character traits. Halberstam writes of
Johnson's untempered and restless appetite for achievement, his need to control everything around him through
attention to detail, and his demand for total loyalty from
his followers: "I want him to kiss my ass in Macy's at
high noon and tell me it smells like roses..." (p. 526). To
Halberstam, Johnson was a ruffian, a gargantuan figure
of primal force. Halberstam called attention to Johnson's
lifelong addiction to politics. He never read a book or
articles on anything but his political activities, he knew
nothing of the pop culture around him. "Who the hell is
Lana Turner?" he asked an aide when as Senate majority
leader he was told he had to go to a press conference
with a movie star (p. 533).

Halberstam's scrupulously detailed comments deal
with Johnson's persona from a sociological viewpoint.
He saw Johnson as a frontier man from Texas in the
company of the sophisticated, urbane elite of the East-
ern establishment, driven to excessive combativeness
to overcome his everpresent experience of ineptitude
around the self-assured old boys of Yale and Harvard.
The vantage point that is lacking in this otherwise pene-
trating volume is the perspective of the intrapsychic
focus.

Halberstam's sociological bias leads him to state that, "there was no doubt ever in his family that he would go to college..." (p. 537). Yet we know from other observers of Johnson that he was mightily resistant toward higher learning (Kearns, Caro, Steinberg) and he fought against entering college for 4 years after high school. Halberstam points out quite correctly that Johnson's mother pushed to ensure his success in precollege schools. But what Halberstam leaves out is the mixture of animus and neediness in Johnson that fueled his lifelong defenses against the "giving woman," so that he allowed himself to take only limited gratification from women, and never allowed any woman to "own" him.

In Halberstam's otherwise rich description of Johnson what is missing is a perception of Johnson's self-deficits, his emptiness, his loneliness, and his constant agitation, coupled with his fears of unfolding himself in a human encounter.

Halberstam does a comprehensive job of detailing Johnson's aspirations and his wish to be the "man of action" in the Vietnam war period. In fact, as Halberstam points out, Johnson was "on a roll" all through the war years.

Halberstam's understanding of Johnson is limited by two determining variables: (1) utilizing the sociological view that Johnson was a man identified with the Texas cowboy values of being a "doer," a "man of action"; and (2) the pseudopsychological view that Johnson was a man whose achievements reflected a mother determined that her youngster would succeed. Each of these psychosocial determinants is of value. But neither is an accurate representation of Johnson's total behaviors as he conveyed them to others, such as his wife, several of his biographers, and as they are described by several of his aides.

Lady Bird Johnson related how frightened he became prior to the 1964 convention when she had to buttress his resolve so that he would stand for election as president. He expressed to Doris Kearns his fears of loneliness, especially in the White House. A doer he was, but the activities too often were fueled by fears of criticism from significant people in his surround—such as the charge of being "soft" on Communism—rather than decisions based on the common good, or decisions informed by empathy with the affected people.

Halberstam could not "see" the lonely, empty self behind the actions—the actions taken to ensure that the important critics and their criticisms be kept to a minimum. In sum, Halberstam's account of Johnson is an exhaustive rounding up of his behaviors which is not then used—nor is it intended to be—to go *beyond* the behaviors for their meanings, in an attempt to understand *what* evoked the actions Johnson took in war and in peace. Halberstam's study, carefully crafted as it is, falls short of a complete picture of Johnson, as do Caro's painstaking descriptions in the absence of a psychological overview. We are left to make what we will of the outward manifestations of Johnson in the behavior so meticulously recorded. What does the behavior *represent?* What did Johnson's incessant need to maintain secrecy stand for? Was it shame, fear of criticism, lack of trust?

Alfred Steinberg's "Sam Johnson's Boy" (1968) is a hard-nosed indictment of Johnson as a man who:

> had learned how to seize authority from the lazy or slow, threaten and storm at the weak, flatter the vain, promise the greedy, buy off the stubborn, and isolate the strong (p. 838). He

had "grown up poor and spent his lifetime fighting for personal wealth and power and in his unquenchable thirst for both failed to acquire any other purpose to guide his decisions" (p. 858) he had been "unable to do what almost all his predecessors had—to grow in office" (p. 839). He was a "man apart without the most important presidential ingredient, the ability to inspire others and gain the affection and trust of the people" (p. 837). In this "Johnson rivaled Herbert Hoover as the twentieth century president most unable to establish a warm relationship with the citizens of the nation." (p. 837)

Steinberg's 839 pages of the facts of Johnson's life are the most detailed of the biographies, representing hundreds of interviews and offering reams of examples of Johnson's interactional world from his earliest years. But Steinberg's work also bypasses the psychological view: Johnson was driven to conquer not just because he was poor, his life of bombast was in great measure a defense against inability to derive nurturance in the ordinary way, the expression of need to a responsive source.

Ronnie Dugger's investigations of Johnson's life in *The Politician* (1982) offer an exposition of Johnson's activities as an entrepreneur, power broker, and political deal maker that is unique in its detail and scope. Dugger offers convincing documentation that Johnson's entire life—in business as in politics—was "marred" by his relentless activity in adjusting to whatever was required to further his search for power.

Dugger chronicles Johnson's rise to the status of multimillionaire (with wealth estimated at 14 million dollars when he became President) by the acquisition of an empire of Texas radio stations, utilizing his influence as congressman to obtain the F.C.C. certification, and then further utilizing his credentials as a congressman to obtain advertising affiliations with national radio networks.

Dugger also documents Johnson's rise to power in the political arena through his knack of self-adjustment to the politics and politicians who could propel him forward to power. Because he was not impeded by ideals or conscience, shame and guilt, he could easily discard one "allegiance" and move on to another, more advantageous affiliation.

Another manifestation of Johnson's adherence to self-interest was his abandonment of the interests of the hill country farmers in his district to serve the interests of the oil and construction companies. Johnson devoted himself in the Congress to the interests of the Brown and Root Construction Company and, through them, other business interests. These people financed his campaigns, offered him the perquisites of private airplanes and luxury hotel suites, and became his business advisers.

Dugger offers several vignettes of Johnson's ability as congressman and senator to enter into skullduggery without being conflicted. One such case was the prospective appointment of Leland Olds to preside over the Federal Power Commission in 1949. Johnson helped pillory this competent public official, whose only sin was that he once was "socialist-minded" and wanted the federal government to regulate natural gas prices. Johnson's friends in the oil and gas industries of course wanted Olds neutralized, and Johnson was all ready to do the dirty work. Olds, he said, would be a commissar, not a commissioner. In fact, Dugger suggests that Senator Joe McCarthy might have picked up cues for red-baiting from watching Johnson defame Olds.

In Evans and Novak's *Lyndon B. Johnson: The Exercise of Power* (1966), the reader is given an entry into the back rooms and cloakrooms where policies and reputations are made and broken. Evans and Novak's book is an striking example of the journalist's craft in providing the reader with details of the exercise of power. Their reportage of the canny tactics of Johnson as congressman, as senator, and as president is mesmerizing in its depiction of the brilliant campaigns which LBJ fought to acquire power. They take the reader into a typical "Johnson treatment" for the persuasion of a fellow legislator with such rendition of Johnson's barrage of language and gestures that one can feel Johnson's hot breath suffusing his victim. They chronicle in their meticulous fashion the battles Johnson fought, lost, and won getting to the Senate and, ultimately, to the position of majority leader, arguably the scene of his greatest triumphs. They focus on the battle plans and guiding principles Johnson adopted:

1. *Attention to detail.* Johnson was usually the best-prepared man in any meeting, or on any panel or committee in which he participated. He knew the tax laws or the bombing targets or whatever was on the agenda to be discussed in any forum.

2. *Emphasis on secrecy.* Johnson would give up a sound proposal rather than allow it to become public. He would become agitated if proposals he wished to remain secret were disclosed. Walter Heller, the chairman of the Council of Economic Advisers, had proposed a daring use of tax revenue—a tax-return scheme to state governments, perhaps with a restriction clause so that it could be limited to use for education. Heller leaked his scheme selectively, ostensibly as a method to encourage interest and/or discussion in Washington. Johnson was so peeved that he removed the plan from active consideration by the White House.

As president, Johnson began using the same methods of secrecy and duplicity that had been so successful in the Senate. These methods soon earned the "credibility gap" label that hounded him throughout his public life and especially in the presidency. Evans and Novak labeled his approach "government by indirection" (p. 502) and cited several examples of Johnson's deviousness which included: lying about cabinet dismissals and appointments (the Yarmolinsky case, the Hodges case) and lying about policy shifts (budget ceilings).

3. *Producing a crisis or a dramatic situation.* Johnson relished theatrical staging. He believed he was more credible if he headed a government that was in crisis or engaged in periodic dramatic moves. Announcements not only were shrouded in secrecy, but issued at shrewdly chosen times, for example at night instead of in the afternoon. He was accused of exaggerating threatening conditions so that the United States could intervene in the affairs of a foreign country, the Dominican Republic, for example. He was accused of distorting the actual events in Tonkin Bay on August 2, 1964, so that the United States could enlarge its military intervention.

4. *Whatever works, use it and ideologies be damned.* Johnson quickly changed political colors in the Senate from being a New Dealer, and from emphasizing interest in the "little man," to becoming a conservative with palm open to the big money of oil and gas interests, real estate interests, and construction companies.

Evans and Novak's contributions to the Johnson story are restricted to reporting Johnson's actions, not to their psychological determinants. When they approach these areas they stick to off-the-cuff summaries: "Johnson was not that type of man," "Johnson was peeved," "Johnson became sullen," and similar comments. Their valuable book is, like almost all of the literature on Johnson, without a deeper interpretation of the man, without speculation on the underlying forces at work.

In the view of Tom Wicker (1968), Johnson's decisions as president were predetermined by the "interplay of personality and circumstance; it was not the mastery of man over event but the yielding of choice to instinct" (p. 275). Johnson drifted into a war that destroyed *him*, his "great society" plans, his visions for the future, and, in a way, his entire life-plan of power-seeking. Wicker describes the tragedy of the Vietnam war as a particular set of tragic actions which Johnson was *compelled* to take. The compulsion stemmed, in Wicker's terms, from Johnson's being always the *politician intent on maintaining consensus* in whatever he did, wherever he went (the omnipresent need for validation). Yet this could only alienate both hawks and doves, as well as the American electorate, who had clearly been on his side because of his masterly performance directly after the shattering event of Kennedy's assassination.

Then, in his first address to a stunned and bereft nation, his mien was meetly diffident, benignant, paternal. Expectations were stirred in a people grateful for solace. Here he was, finally a national leader, not just a Southerner; and a "good" person, rather than a self-seeking, money-grabbing, power-hungry provincial. He had soothed the fears of the American people, telling them over and over by implication and directly that he would *not* send American boys to fight in Asia. No sooner did he become president, than the game plan for the bombing of Vietnam was unfurled, on February 7, 1965. Of course, the Tonkin Bay Resolution had already been operative since August 1964, when it was passed by Congress. This resolution, the operational declaration of war in Vietnam, gave Johnson war powers after North Vietnamese patrol boats "attacked" the American destroyers (the *Maddox* and the *C. Turner Joy*) twice in succession in Tonkin Bay.

As countless observers, including Wicker, have pointed out, Johnson was indecisive about the extent of the bombing. He had to consider the effect on China; would they come to the aid of North Vietnam? He was also under political constraint not to allow an all-out war. He found a middle ground in the retaliatory bombing which he ordered on February 7, 1965 after a Vietcong attack on an American Special Forces base. This date marks the point at which war can be said to have begun in Vietnam.

After the retaliatory bombing began, ground troops were necessary to maintain security for the air forces; and soon our armies were used in actual combat. In reaction to these decisions, spurred, in Wicker's terms, by the confluence of events and by his own circumstances, in addition to the political considerations — Johnson became one of the most unpopular presidents in American history. He was unsuccessful in war and "unable to mobilize in his people the spirit of sacrifice and commitment needed if any modern nation is to support a modern war" (p. 272).

Wicker's view of Johnson is confined to the biological and the behavioral. He conceives of Johnson as a man of the South in whom the heritage of Ol' Massa had been overcome but not forgotten. "He was and is a man of power and pride, and the latter will not brook much hindrance of the former, particularly from men who though not perhaps inferior still have to be reminded

from time to time of the realities of things" (p. 252). In
Wicker's view, Johnson was not about to let little brown
men who skulked in the jungle take over "his" front
porch, the symbol for what Johnson conceived of as his
world of power.

In an invaluable set of reflections on Johnson as
president, Hugh Sidey (1968), then a Washington reporter, made clear what Johnson demonstrated to the
press people who followed him daily at the White House
and to far-off places. He practiced sleight-of-hand to the
extent that reporters coined the term the "credibility
gap." He could look Sidey in the face and say Richard
Goodwin was not his speech writer and then, a few
weeks later, brag that "Goodwin can write a better
speech than Sorensen and in one-fifth the time" (p. 160).

In Sidey's view, Johnson's dilemma as president
stemmed from his difficulty in transforming himself
from legislator to chief executive. The president needs
candor and consistency, not "Johnson's tricky footwork"
(p. 170), lying about his proposed budget, lying about
staff appointments, and lying about his tastes in alcoholic beverages (scotch, not bourbon).

He became ludicrous in describing his rationale—
later proved false—for sending 24,000 troops into the
Dominican Republic to quell a relatively minor distur-
bance: "Some fifteen hundred innocent people were
murdered and shot and their heads cut off..." (p. 178).
Charges about Johnson's credibility began to mount as
he struggled to create the false impression that he was
not going to war in the spring of 1965, when he had
already committed hundreds of thousands of troops to
the battle.

As Sidey cites by chapter and verse, credibility became the biggest problem in Johnson's presidency. "It

tainted in some way almost everything he did" (p. 194).
Sidey also noted that Johnson had no insight into the
part he played in interactions with the press and,
through them, with the country. He asked plaintively:
"Why should Ho Chi Minh believe me when the newspapers and the networks in my own country don't believe me?" (p. 195). But while exhaustively documenting
Johnson's compulsions for secrecy, for exaggerations to
justify actions, for image-building rituals, Sidey though
often bemused and, occasionally, outraged, proposed
no interpretations of Johnson's background data and of
the determinants of his behavior. Johnson is merely described as attempting to be "omnipotent," or as "ridicu-
lous," and one who "could not break himself of his
habits" (p. 188).

Frank Cormier (1977), the representative from the
Associated Press who was with Johnson, declares he
"often admired" Johnson. But his book runs true to
form in the genre of Johnson biographies; a documentation of an outrageous, brilliant, and devious man. The
games of secrecy and double-dealing are once again
minutely documented, with some additions but without reflection on the determinants of Johnson's character. As soon as LBJ assumed the presidency, he told the
inner group of reporters traveling with him on Air Force
One that he and the White House Press Corps could
"establish a mutual aid society" (p. 5). As Cormier remembered Johnson's words: "If you help me, I'll help
you. I'll make you-all big men in your profession" (p. 5).
When Cormier tried to disabuse him of this concept,
Johnson was surprised at the notion that there might not
be perpetual amity between the press and himself.
Again amply evident in Cormier's book is Johnson's im-

periousness, his inability to be empathic, and his vulnerability to criticism or rebuff.

THE HISTORIANS AND PHILOSOPHERS

In *Modern Times* (1983), Paul Johnson argues in a chapter entitled "America's Suicide Attempt" that the Vietnam war was a suicide attempt almost successfully executed by three presidents, all of good intention: Eisenhower, Kennedy, and Johnson. Eisenhower, in Paul Johnson's view, was the most liable for the tragedy. When France signed a cease-fire agreement at Geneva in July 1954, the provisions divided the country into two spheres of influence and further specified that free elections were to take place in two years from the date of the armistice. The premier of the South, Ngo Dinh Diem (later executed by people in the pay of President Kennedy) did not abide by the Geneva accord. Eisenhower did not sign the accords and did not pressure Diem to abide by them.

Paul Johnson's argument is that allowing free elections to take place might have resulted in a victory for Ho Chi Minh, the President of North Vietnam, who would have become the ruler of a unified Communist country; but that this would *not* have been a disaster to the United States. Eisenhower—the author of the "domino theory," which postulated that other countries in Southeast Asia would become Communist as soon as Indo-China was swallowed up—of course disagreed, and therefore acquiesced in Diem's refusal to submit to the test of the polls. Here Eisenhower departed from American global policy. The Vietcong emerged three years after the default of the election process and by 1959 a new war started in the south.

Kennedy's sin consisted of dispatching 7,000 troops to aid the South Vietnam forces, thus sinking the United States deeper into the quagmire. Finally Kennedy secretly authorized support for a coup, and Diem was murdered, with American support highly visible (the CIA was reported to have given $42,000 to the Vietnamese officers who then set up a military junta to become the leaders of South Vietnam).

After Johnson became president, the first aggressive act he initiated in Vietnam was the retaliatory bombing after the Tonkin Bay affair, ostensibly to demonstrate his strength of purpose in not deserting the South Vietnamese. These bombings in August 1964 effectively became the start of the Vietnam war. Paul Johnson believes that, having initiated the bombing, Lyndon Johnson should have occupied the North, in effect. But he remained indecisive. The U.S. Air Force strategists declared that they could win if the bombing was swift, and was repeated over and over without restraint. That was, after all, the military lesson of World War II.

However, Johnson's bombing tactics were always political to avert criticism by China, Russia, the U.S. Congress, and critics from the left. In Paul Johnson's view, because the bombing intensified slowly, the Vietnamese had ample time to build shelters and to adjust. When Russia agreed to build missile installations, Johnson ordered the bombers not to attack these installations. Moreover, there were sixteen bombing pauses — none of which evoked any initiative to negotiate. Of course, the North Vietnamese were not deterred by the casualties, those suffered or meted out. Self-imposed restraints of bombing and ground action proved useless and were interpreted as lack of courage in contrast to Ho Chi Minh's intransigence.

On the home front, LBJ was losing—and finally lost—the propaganda war. At first the press backed him, including the liberal *New York Times* and *Washington Post,* each of which agreed that South Vietnam should be supported. But by 1966 and 1967, the press became antagonistic to Johnson and the Vietnam adventure and called for a withdrawal of all troops. Actually, the media originally was strongly biased in its presentation and was misled. The photos of prisoners thrown out of planes were staged. Other damaging stories were inaccurate, such as the accounts of American prisoners contained in "tiger cages."

The American leadership began to crumble soon after the great and final Vietcong offensive—the Tet offensive on January 30, 1968. In actuality, the Vietcong army suffered mightily in the Tet offensive and it failed in its attempts to evoke a mass uprising of the people in the south. The propaganda payoff in the United States was great, however, as Americans had been assured that the Vietcong had lost their effectiveness and that the South Vietnamese armies were becoming more effective and reclaiming more and more villages previously lost to the Vietcong.

Although the vast majority of Americans continued to back the war (support for withdrawal never reached more than 20 percent), the American leadership lost its direction after the Tet offensive. The leaders who now turned against the war included many formerly identified as "hawkish": Dean Acheson, Clark Clifford, William Fulbright, Arthur Goldberg, and Robert McNamara. Another blow to LBJ and the war came in March 1968 when Secretary of the Treasury Henry Fowler protested that dispersing any additional troops would compromise existing domestic programs, and that American finances were not limitless.

To turn to the Great Society programs, Paul Johnson's view is that, in perspective, many facets of the enterprise were unsuccessful. For example, the attack on poverty proved deadly to the maintenance of the poor family—the welfare laws made it pay for these families to split up. Another project that proved misguided was the attack on educating the poor; the spending increased but the educational performance failed. Another of Johnson's illusions was that, with his increasing success in securing black rights, would come more harmony between blacks and the city and federal governments. The opposite occurred. Two weeks after the Civil Rights Bill was passed in July 1964, the first of the great black riots erupted in Harlem and Brooklyn. The culmination of black anger came in Los Angeles with the Watts riot, which lasted for six days and claimed a death toll of 34, with $200 million worth of property destroyed.

In Paul Johnson's view, by the time LBJ handed the presidency over to Richard Nixon, it was clear that he had lost the support of the people in many areas. The war, the economy, the great social programs—none had been successful, although all had been launched with high confidence.

Paul Conklin's historical biography *Big Daddy from the Pedernales* (1986) offered a version of Johnson as a man caught in a trap: He desperately wished to succeed as the commander in a successful war and as the great leader of a society determined to cure all of its ills, poverty and inequality among the most important. However, Johnson was unable to succeed in his quest for military and social victory because of the personal devils of secrecy and duplicity which he unconsciously inserted as mechanisms to avoid failure.

He covered up too much, and as soon as colleagues and critics realized the extent of his commitment to Vietnam in men and dollars, he was attacked on all sides. When his peace initiatives failed, Johnson could only look forward to resigning. On March 31, 1968, Johnson announced that he would not stand for reelection, but would devote his remaining tenure as president to work for peace. Peace did not come to him either, and he left the office, as Conkin put it, "defeated and disgraced" (p. 290).

Conkin's volume contributes a lucid sweep of many of the events preceding and during the war. On the other hand, in his attempt to comprehend Johnson, especially in his relationship to his parents, Conkin resists facing the manifest data so as to reach a partial understanding of Johnson. Lyndon Johnson was, as Conkin describes him, a troubled man, and his decisions in peace and war reflected these "troubles." Conkin makes clear that Johnson's judgment was affected because his "sense of well-being was tied so closely to achievement and the gratitude of his constituents, he could never for long gain any sense of self-acceptance or peace" (p. 174).

As Conkin continues, "He kept trying harder and harder, pushing ever more futilely towards the ever-retreating goal of respect and popularity" (p. 174). Without stating it directly, Conkin describes what is to us a major difficulty in Johnson's leadership—his limited capacity for empathy, to feel the other's pain. In fact, as Conkin describes from his readings (he interviewed no one), Johnson was not honest, he denied facts, he loved to torment reporters. In a word, he could not be trusted. In Conkin's account of Johnson's behavior during the war, he makes it clear that Johnson's interest was only in victory, a magical strategy that would fill him with omnipotence. But Johnson became a stumbling giant who was "anything but noble," he "had played the bully," and "flaunted his achievements," so that the multitudes were not "inclined to cry," but "openly or secretly to rejoice" at his fall from power (p. 194).

CRITICAL ANALYSIS

To the psychohistorian, the observations cited here are from one view and of one piece. They offer descriptions of Johnson's behavior, his decisions, his episodes of disarray, and his insatiable need to be admired. Some observers (White, 1964; Wicker, 1968) would take his behaviors to be derived from class identifications with Texas, and with poverty. Others (Conkin, 1986) indicate traits stemming from genetic endowments. Still other observers would take his behavior to be the outcome of overindulgence, the "spoiled brat" explanation of obduracy or self-centeredness (Conkin, 1986; Steinberg, 1968). Many observers expressed their negative reactions either directly (Cormier, 1977; Sidey, 1968; Steinberg, 1968) or obliquely (Caro, 1983; Dugger, 1982) or in a manner that can be described as *studied* (Paul Johnson, 1983). Conversely, there are those observers whose admiration is direct (William White, 1964) or implied (Conkin, 1986).

In sum, the data from the observers who wrote about Johnson from a distance offer provocative material on his behavior and even more on how people reacted to him. But beyond the manifest, beyond the idealization, and beyond the transferential still hides the inner self of

Lyndon Johnson, which to perceive for what it is requires deeper probing.

SUMMARY OF CHAPTERS 2 AND 3

At the close of these two chapters centered on collating the existing descriptions of Lyndon Johnson,
findings emerge that can be added up to delineate a
profile of his self similar to the empathic diagnosis
made at the beginning of a psychotherapy. These findings fit several categories:

1. *The conflict-free sphere of the self; genetic endowments.*
Johnson was always known for his high intelligence
manifested in his prodigious memory and in his ability
to comprehend information quickly and accurately. He
could also shut out interfering stimuli easily and concentrate for long periods. He often asserted that he
could turn off consciousness and ease into sleep, of
which he needed only three or four hours. (He did take
a daily nap after his heart attack.)

2. *The pole of ambitions of Johnson's self.*
Every observer and student of Johnson marveled at
his assertiveness in behavior, reflecting an unneutralized
ambitiousness, or a nearly unneutralized pole of ambitions, including his spouse. Only his friend-reporter
William White could not psychologically "see" Johnson, since his vision was obscured by his idealization.
"What's for me" was not a song Johnson sang to convey a
wish for egalitarian relationships. His ambitious needs
fueled each aspect of his life. To get ahead, not to be left
behind, to be in charge, to be recognized, all these strivings reflected the urgency of his yearning for admiration and applause, *now*. This neediness was always

acknowledged by his observers as the manifestations of a demanding man. Another aspect of this drive that was never recognized was that it never could be gratified. Johnson was never content for any length of time. What we are looking at here is not the behaviors of a formed man with egregious traits. We are witnessing the intrusion into the adult self of a youngster, an ungratified and demanding infant self, crying out for the unattained and unattainable nurturance of a caretaker. Episodes of repetitious demandingness in adults reflect infantile fixations and therefore are never capable of gratification in adulthood. Such strivings can only be illuminated (made conscious) in psychotherapy so that, over time, their impact on the adult self and adult functioning diminishes.

3. *Narcissistic balance in the self.*

Narcissistic deficit—low self-worth, ordinarily accompanied by a sense of emptiness and loneliness—plagued Johnson throughout his life. This finding was described most vividly by his biographer Doris Kearns. Johnson's endogenous stores of self-value and self-calming we have to surmise were always inadequate. Many observers described his constant need for company—even to go to the washroom. Conversely, when Johnson did win extraordinary accolades or applause, or when a project scored a major success, the triumph was often received with such excitement or even disarray, that he became too "high." Johnson's narcissistic balance was not well modulated. He could soar from the depths of despair to heights of ebullience. Again, this instability indicates that the endogenous self-worth in his self was meager. He was always in need of a new infusion of worth. For example, as we have previously documented, just prior to the 1964 Democratic Convention, he told Lady Bird he would not run because he feared rejection. Thus, even at a time when fortune smiled, he was still prone to attacks of lowered self-worth. An example of the overstimulation of his self occurred when the Dominican crisis was over, and, in his jubilance he extolled the Secretary-General of the Organization of American States:

> That Jose Mora did a wonderful job for our country. He did such a wonderful job, he can have anything I've got. He can have my little daughter Luci. Why I'd even tongue him myself. (Cormier, p. 190)

Johnson both craved the narcissistic input—the sign of deprivation from infancy (the failed self/selfobject encounter)—and became fearful when it was precipitously given to him—the sign of fear of the giver (selfobject) from infancy.

4. *The pole of values and the internalized calming-soothing functions.*

When Lyndon Johnson came into a room, no one was unaware of this entrance. Not only was there an immediate "attack" on whomever was closest to his person, a touch, or a grab, or two hands on your lapels and the 6'3" (closer to 6'4") giant's face a few millimeters from yours, speaking in an outpouring of words and excited affect. Apart from the manifest demand for mirroring (applause, or other forms of admiration) another important finding is that the self of Johnson was a self in dire need of calming, and yet was unable to utilize the human encounter to achieve the experience of equanimity. He was always on the go: whether it was in reading a document, finishing your thought before you did, eating as if it was a contest to finish first, sleeping no more than three to four hours a night. His staff, idealizing him as they did, started to emulate him in what became known as "the Johnson trot." He had, in sum, a psychomotor speedup (hyperkinesis) and diminished self-worth (Caro, 1983, p. 456).

Johnson required calming and soothing from his surround until the end of his days because he had no endogenous self-calming resources. These comprise the interiorized functions of the idealized parent, whose imago (memory trace) ordinarily becomes permanently implanted into the self of the infant. Usually this takes place before the age of before six months. Johnson's self was deficient in this regard. He had little on which to draw in the way of self-calming and self-soothing functions.

Another major aspect of the process of achieving intrapsychic peace is the capacity to derive these comforts within the human encounter. Those who cannot achieve a human bond to secure intrapsychic peace have to turn to work, to gambling, to drugs, to achieve the calm of eventual fatigue from work or of sedation through drugs. Johnson's life of hyperactivity and inability to achieve peace from human relationships made clear that his infancy and childhood with his selfobject parents did not provide the necessary calming, and because of this deprivation, manufactured his fixation—the repetitious seeking behavior for external sources of calming.

The second far-reaching effect of the failure of the idealized parent function was that, although Johnson reached out for some words and actions to calm and soothe him from different people, his capacity to sink into any relationship over time and derive a measure of calm was limited. "Just so much" and "just so far" were tacit caveats demarcating his interpersonal encounters.

The other facet of the idealized parent function is to provide directions and guidance, which results in the internalization of codes to ensure a self that acts from an established base of morality and with a set of established standards (values) for a person within a certain culture. Once again, these aspects of the idealized self-object caretaker of childhood are ordinarily interiorized early in life, however different facets of a parent's attitudes are added to the self throughout childhood and adolescence.

Johnson's never-ending quest for direction and guidance was one of the most striking aspects of his persona, as he dived into a gross identification with his father's swagger and talk in his early teens, and later "became" President Cecil Evans in college, and then "became" in succession FDR, Sam Rayburn, and Richard Russell. People remarked how quiet he was around Russell, how much of a Texas drawl he assumed with Rayburn, how jaunty he was around FDR. And again, the intrapsychic and tacit motto was "just so far," since he could and did easily replace these seemingly permanent mergers with others as a frequent happenstance. The intrapsychic restrictions that did not allow him to stay with the ideals of FDR or Russell or whoever was his current "political daddy" were of course the experiences of rejection from his early days at the hands of those whose leadership was not consistent or not consistently benevolent; so that dependency was always a tentative and a time-limited enterprise for Johnson.

The important finding that resulted from the failures of Johnson's selfobject caretakers was that he did not have the unconscious and therefore automatic regulators in his pole of values of a morality code, a set of standards and values by which to posture himself. His "morality code" was in reality not a code that would make him experience *guilt* over transgression; nor did he have a set of standards that made him experience *shame*. He could and did harm others, he did lie, he was duplicitous. All this and much more in the way of amoral behavior he exhibited without the inner restraints that would be evoked by empathy.

5. *Johnson's interpersonal relationships.*

Johnson had few genuine peer relationships in which dialogue and trust are the major ingredients. His so-called friends were ultimately used for some project or other purpose of his. The so-called "close" friends— Fortas, Judge Moursand, and others—were friends *over* an area in which they provided some benefit for Johnson, advice, or direction, or something of value to him.

Indeed, most of his relationships were of the archaic self/selfobject variety, in which the significant other offered the mirroring, or the calming, or direction of the idealized parent—always time-limited. These relationships were the ones he entered into with Cecil Evans, Sam Rayburn, Alvin Wirtz, Richard Russell, Charles Marsh, and Herman Brown.

Johnson himself also became the idealized selfobject in many of his relations as a by product of his fear of his own passivity and his resulting assumption of command or control. Apart from those he directly impacted upon in his family and staff—Lady Bird and Jack Valenti are representatives in this category—there were countless others with whom he interacted daily who pedestallized him.

Johnson's interactions with people did not include empathy. Experiencing the other's fear or chagrin or sorrow or hunger did not influence his rebellion in adolescence to quell his mother's concerns; thus, he did not hesitate to crow after he removed Bobby Kennedy from his choices as a vice-presidential candidate for the 1964 election.

6. *The other self functions of Lyndon Johnson.*

The other findings from the accumulated data point to other deficits in the self functions of Johnson. The absence of empathy which we have already observed is part of an overall lack in the self-observing functions seen in L.B.J. Other self functions that were not operating in a modal way were his capacity to neutralize aggression, and the maintenance of a well-formed repression barrier. When disappointed with someone's actions, or confronted by an error committed, he would be unable to inhibit the egress of hostility or to neutralize the anger. He would lapse into partial or total disarray. The torrent of abuse that an error or critical comment would trigger was so primitive in nature that it rendered most observers unable to respond. Here again we are witness not to an "ugly" side of Johnson's "nature." We are witness to a deficit in the interiorization of those mechanisms which ordinarily are interiorized as identifications with the caretaker selfobjects. These constitute the end result of relationships with ever-present, consistent, and benevolent parents with whom one can easily identify.

7. *Reactions to rejection, repudiation, criticism, and malevolent behaviors.*

Johnson's fear of criticism and rejection was among his best-known traits and undoubtedly the one from which he suffered the most. He so feared elections, a potential source of repudiation, that he either became ill in anticipation or threatened not to run. In 1968, he actually withdrew from the election. His fear of possible criticism at times became so fierce that he became near-violent when his associates and staff blundered, and thereby left him open to potential attack.

His reactions to rejection also included counterattacks; when he received criticism for his overreaction in the Dominican Republic incident, he invented an outlandish story of beheadings. When so many turned against him during the Vietnam war, he often accused people of being unpatriotic or of siding with the Communists.

He often attacked with sadistic outbursts of derisive commentaries or "jokes" at others' expense.

What we view here is, again, the diminished self-regard or self-value which Johnson's self contained. Unfortunately for him and for everyone else, Johnson's reaction to rebuff was overwhelming, since he agreed for the most part, unconsciously — with the overt, covert, or imagined decision that he was, in some way, feckless, wanting, and inept.

Chapter 4

WHERE DOES IT COME FROM?

ON THE SEARCH FOR THE DETERMINING FACTORS IN LYNDON JOHNSON'S SELF

The student of mankind, whether studying great figures who influenced the world in their time or a patient
in our consultation suites, must be concerned with
those influences from the past that have influenced the
development of the personality under scrutiny. The goal
of psychohistorians is first to uncover the crucial data
that will enable them finally to recognize the significant
people in the person's background and the person's significant experiences. These should include those experiences that resulted in special qualities or structures of
the subject being studied.

Similarly, clinical investigators strive to uncover
significant events and significant people in the patient's
background before they attempt to perform their thera-
peutic task. The difference between the two kinds of

investigators at this stage is the kind of data available for each line of investigation. The clinician has the patient's remembrances; the psychohistorian may have the subject's remembrances told to biographers, as well as accounts by outside observers of a variety of aspects of the person's life that may illuminate different influences on the subject's development.

After obtaining initial background information, clinical investigators check, and alter, if necessary, these initial historical impressions over and over again with the patient as allusions (i.e., free associations) are made to significant events or people from his background. Moreover, he will be able to assign more and more clearly over time the valence of importance of the various historical events and personages on the ongoing personality and its problems. In this way an interpersonal encounter with a particular person in the patient's present life will be found to be connected through the associations to a series of encounters with a caretaker of the past that was significant in forming an area of sensitivity.

This method of assessing the important aspects of background influences through present to past linkages is a well-known and cardinal diagnostic feature of psychoanalytic treatment. Once the psychoanalyst begins to interpret his findings to the patient of these past-to-present linkages, the working-through phase of the therapy is begun. After a significant amount of interpretative work is accomplished, the past-to-present transferences are illuminated and diminished and the patient begins to recover from victimization by his past.

The psychohistorian's approach, on the other hand, is necessarily based on other people's observations of the different figures and events in the subject's background. Since psychohistorians cannot "see" the patient's formed self in relation to past persons and events, and there are no free associations framing the unconscious connections in an interview from present to past, he has to *surmise* that a subject's revealed unique behaviors are in part reenactments—the unconscious repeating of wishes, defenses, sensitivities, and disappointments from the past.

Further psychohistorians, attempting to assign valence onto different aspects of the subject's background without the benefit of a session of associations from past-to-present material, have to rely on sequences within the biographical material in order to make the connections between past and present. Such might be the mother's pregnancy, followed by a self transformation in the youngster from a quiet child to a clamoring, never-pleased trouble-seeker.

The psychohistorian also has to rely on certain developmental schemas and psychological tasks to be mastered in a modal self. Thus he asks: What data are available from observers of Johnson's first year of life which will attest to the mirroring qualities of the mother, Rebekah Baines Johnson? What data are there to reveal what was going on in the family at the time he began to run away from home as a child of four? In short, what data are available to assess his self development—the successes and failures—through his childhood and adolescence?

JOHNSON'S EARLY CHILDHOOD

To those who knew the Johnsons, including those who were part of the family, Lyndon was his mother's favorite, even though she had four other children: Rebekah (two years younger), Josepha (four years younger), Sam Houston (six years younger), and Lucia (eight years younger). This testimony came from his mother (Rebekah Baines Johnson, 1965), his brother (Sam Johnson, 1970), and from his various biographers (Caro, 1983; Kearns, 1976; Steinberg, 1968). His mother, Rebekah Baines Johnson (1965), described Lyndon's birth:

> Now the light came in from the east bringing a deep stillness, stillness so profound and so pervasive that it seemed as if the earth itself were listening. And there came a sharp, compelling cry—the most awesome, happiest sound known to human ears—the cry of a newborn baby; the first child of Sam Ealy and Rebekah Johnson was "discovering America." (p. 17)

Rebekah Baines Johnson's enthusiasm for her new baby was further evident in her response to her husband's photograph of their six-month-old infant. She reports that as Sam raised up the photo she "ran to meet him in the middle of the Brenner pasture to exclaim rapturously over the photograph of our boy" (p. 32).

So intent was she that her son acquire the proper literary and artistic values that she taught him the alphabet well before his second birthday. They would while away the time lying in bed with Rebekah reading Lyndon her literary favorites, which included Browning and Milton, the Bible, and Greek and Roman mythology. Disappointed that her husband lacked the appreciation for high culture that she had grown to love at her father's knee, she turned to her firstborn hopeful that he could be a companion to share the "higher things" (Kearns, 1976, p. 22). Her well-read father had been a lawyer, a state legislator, and a lay preacher. Her grandfather had been president of Baylor University. She had in fact been raised in a family that was attuned to aesthetic values.

Dark clouds appeared on the horizon when her father, Joseph Baines, during her final college years at Baylor, entered into an ill-fated financial deal from which he never recovered, financially or emotionally. Prior to his death, he introduced his daughter to a fellow legislator, Samuel Ealy Johnson. The couple saw each other for several years and married after her father's death in August, 1907. Rebecca's reduced financial circumstances and the emotional unavailability of her husband made her turn to her firstborn for comfort. Johnson mentioned often and with emphasis that he had a special role to play in maintaining his mother's psychic equilibrium, even in his earliest years (Kearns, 1976). To Doris Kearns (1976) he commented:

> There was nothing Mother hated more than seeing my daddy drink. When he had too much to drink, he'd lose control of himself. He used bad language. He squandered the little money we had on the cotton and real estate markets. Sometimes he'd be lucky and make a lot of money. But more often he lost out. One year we'd all be riding high in Pedernales terms, so high in fact that on a scale of A to F, we'd be right up there with the A's. Then two years later, he'd lose it all. The cotton he had bought for forty-four cents a bale had dropped to six cents a bale, and with it the Johnsons had dropped to the bottom of the heap. These ups and downs were hard on my mother. She wanted things to be nice for us, but she could never count on a stable income. When she got upset, she blamed our money problems on my father's drinking. And then she cried a lot. Especially when he stayed out all night. I remembered one bad night. I woke up and heard her in the parlor crying her eyes out. I knew she needed me. With me there, she seemed less afraid. She stopped crying and told me over and over how important it was that I never lose control of myself and disappoint her that way. I promised that I would be there to protect her always. Finally she calmed down and we both fell asleep. (p. 24)

Another reminiscence evidences the special support function that, in Johnson's view, he met for his mother:

> She never wanted me to be alone. She kept me constantly amused. I remember playing games with her that only the two of us could play. And she always let me win even if to do so we had to change the rules. I knew how much she needed me, that she needed me to take care of her. I liked that. It made me feel big and important. It made me believe I could do anything in the whole world. (p. 24)

Among the biographers of Johnson, the consensus is that the bond between him and his mother in early life was fundamentally different from her bond to the other children (Caro, 1983; Kearns, 1976; Steinberg, 1968). The bond, however, had a built-in caveat: Johnson would receive his mother's approval and admiration only so long as he remained the passive listener to her literary and cultural declamations and then parroted these performances. It was also clear that she turned away from supporting the ordinary manifestations of children's play such as shouting, running, and other rowdy behaviors. Not only did Lyndon learn the alphabet before he was two, he read and spelled before he was four, and according to his mother's claim, knew all the Mother Goose rhymes at the age of three. At three he could also recite long passages of poetry from Longfellow and Tennyson (RBJ, 1965).

Johnson treated subordinates in a way that was uncannily similar to the way his mother treated him during this early boyhood phase. A recollection related to Kearns by Johnson provides a primordial version for what was later to become "the Johnson treatment"—a burst of physical demonstrativeness—in this case inflicted by the mother on Johnson:

> I'll never forget how much my mother loved me when I

recited those poems. The minute I finished she'd take me in her arms and hug me so hard I sometimes thought I'd be strangled to death. (Kearns, 1976, p. 25)

Lyndon was also known to be a "restless" infant and child which his mother described in benign terms:

Lyndon from his earliest days possessed a highly inquisitive mind. He was never content to play quietly in the yard. He must set out to conquer that new unexplored world beyond the gate or up the lane. He would be playing in the yard and if his mother turned away for a minute, Lyndon would toddle down the road to see Grandpa. (R. B. Johnson, 1965, p. 5)

However "inquisitive" Lyndon was, his running away became quite a problem for the entire Johnson family. His mother especially was frightened of the nearby Pedernales River and the snakes in the vicinity. Two important events occurred in Johnson's life at the time that his running-away-to-be-caught became a serious problem. His sister Rebekah was born when he was two. Then Rebekah Baines Johnson, quite enervated after her second delivery, took to her bed for several weeks. Since she had always hated the drudgery of routine housework, her husband Sam hired a local girl to come in and clean; her mother also came from San Marcos where she lived (Caro, 1983).

What was Johnson's reaction to his mother's withdrawal? At four he was running away so often his father hung a bell on the porch so his mother could more easily summon help in finding him. One relative, who was a frequent visitor and peer of Johnson's, remarked: "He wanted attention; he would run away and run away...it was all to get attention" (Caro, 1983, p. 68).

Lyndon began to traverse greater and greater distances during his excursions but he would always be found by his mother who, of course, had to leave whatever was occupying her to chase after Lyndon. Also, as the length of his absences became prolonged, Lyndon was surely aware that this would frighten his mother, fearful as she was of the Pedernales River, and the snakes and other wildlife in the neighborhood. At age five an incident occurred, described to Kearns (1976):

> Later that day, I left home to walk to my grandfather's house, which was a half-mile up the road. Mother, always afraid that I would fall into the river, had told me never to leave the dirt path. But the day was hot and the road was dry and dusty and I wanted to cool my hands and feet. I left the road and ran down to the riverbank. I was skipping along until I fell on the roots of a dead tree, and hit my head. I tried to get up. My head hurt. I fell back and lay still. I thought I would be left there forever. It was my punishment. Then, suddenly, my parents were there. Together they picked me up and carried me home. They put me to bed, blew out the light, and sat down at the end of the bed waiting for me to fall asleep. All the time they kept talking in a low voice. They sounded good together. Mother's voice was not as cold as it usually was when she talked to Father. His voice was warm, too. I remember thinking that being hurt and frightened was worth it, so long as it ended this way. I thought that I would have been willing to go through the experience a hundred times to be sure of finding at the end a thing so nice and friendly as my parents were then. (p. 27)

Ironically, it was Johnson's running away that enabled him to enter the local school when he was only four years old, since he was there so often. His mother talked the teacher into allowing him to enter into the school to which he often escaped when he ran away from home (Caro, 1983). The story told by his teacher, Katie Diedrick, has often been cited. She related that Johnson was a frightened four-year-old who displayed infantile behavior requiring caressing to keep him calm (Steinberg, 1968). Johnson was seemingly experiencing a need for nurturance at this time in his life.

As Caro reports (1983) from interviews with relatives and former schoolmates, Johnson's need to be on center stage led him to dress differently from the children of the poor farmers to make himself stand out. When excused to go to the privy he scrawled his name on the blackboard as required, but in giant letters to set himself apart. He had to be the head—first in line, first on the communal donkey, first in games. Friends and relatives as well as schoolmates recognized his need for attention. He had to be the leader and he needed to make sure everyone knew it. No matter what the activity—marbles, baseball, card games—Lyndon had to be first. His cousin said of him at this stage, "He wanted attention. He wanted to be somebody" (Caro, 1983, p. 70).

These data that attest to Lyndon's insistence on garnering whatever attention was available revealed the elemental behaviors in his childhood. After all, he had recently experienced the trauma of the transition from having been the apple of his mother's eye in infancy and early childhood to what must have been experienced by him as being abandoned, cast adrift in the world. This experience of abandonment fueled his incessant exhibitionism and appetite to capture complete attention in each of his relationships. Lyndon continued throughout life his persistent attempts to secure the psychic supplies of mirroring he needed to cover the felt deprivation and emptiness.

Although he continued his efforts to extract nurturance wherever he was, he also attempted to support his emerging self through identification with the men in his life, his paternal grandfather and, later, his father. As is so often the case in those attempting to alleviate failed parental experiences in which compensatory parental figures are not available, or are flawed, the symptoms of the self-worth and self-soothing deficiency persisted. These consisted of the unremitting appetite for support, the vulnerability to insult, the restlessness and agitation so strong that he could not achieve a state of calm sufficient to read without some reminder—a noise, a human voice—that he was not alone.

And so Lyndon Johnson grew through his earliest years hungry for the attention that had been given him at first but then increasingly diminished so that at the age of four he was literally running somewhere each day for recognition. On the other hand, we have many accounts from his mother's and Johnson's remembrances to attest to her emphasis on developing his verbal skills and her instructions in poetry and the classics. She kept him in curls and dresses until his father insisted that the curls be cut, which caused her many tears (Caro, 1983).

All this points to a caretaker who mirrored the intellectual development of her son as well as his decorativeness. What we are describing are the residues of childhood deprivation in the area of self-mirroring and self-calming. At age four, Lyndon was a needy youngster who clamored for recognition and who was overactive and therefore not able to be calm enough to perform with ease the ordinary tasks of a four-year-old. His caretakers did not provide him with sufficient mirroring experiences to allow him to develop enough self-regard not to have to demand succor or its derivatives—winning, being on center stage at all times—wherever and with whoever he was. Similarly, his caretakers did not provide him with sufficient soothing and direction to enable him to feel an inner peace, so that he constantly sought out a patriarchal or matriarchal leader.

Whether these fixations came about as a result of

deprivations from his mother who became increasingly enervated, psychologically and physiologically, with each new child, *or* as a result of being subject to a mother who was always limited in her caretaking, save for her interest in his intellectual development and his decorativeness, cannot be validated either from our sources or *any* observational approach. In psychoanalytic therapy as well as in the observations of the child researchers, the *experiences* of the youngster living through a relationship with the significant caretakers are *never* available to inspection. All we ever have are outcome data from which we make surmises. Lyndon constantly sought mirroring from all in his surround, including his daily attempts to induce his mother to stop her other activities and attend only to him. He was always on a trot and could not be contained or confined. This particular symptom, indicating a deficit in self-calming caused by a paucity of caretaking calmers, resulted in Johnson's lifelong struggle with activities that required him to be "confined" to read and study (e.g., his fear of going to college).

LATER CHILDHOOD AND THE SEARCH FOR A COMPENSATORY CARETAKER

We have adduced from the evidence gathered, including Johnson's behaviors and experiences, that the mirroring from a caretaker did not become sufficiently interiorized in Johnson's self. We now turn to those experiences that may or may not add to the self-regard or compensate for the defective self-regard, the merger with an idealized parent who is a source of calming and soothing, and who instills directives that become firm and power-laden guidelines for life. When these selfobject functions (guiding, directing) become interiorized, the self is enhanced by those interiorized precepts that become firm guidelines throughout life. The self is further enhanced by the internalized calming and soothing, now an endogenous supply of self-calming that permits the self to de-fuse, i.e., to regulate an emerging wave of excitation before the self is overwhelmed. Another important interaction with a caretaker of childhood is the merger with the other's styles of doing life—from walking to throwing a ball to expressing affects—the identification with the significant caretaker's skills and styles (the alter-ego or the twinship merger).

In Johnson's childhood his father and grandfather were the idealized figures to whom he turned for these acquisitions of power and direction, calming and development of skills. The data we have of Sam Ealy Johnson's parenting in the early years of Lyndon's childhood reveal that he was certainly an omnipresent figure of power. He bellowed a great deal, he had a short fuse, he and Rebekah often fought in front of the children (Caro, 1983; Kearns, 1976). The *idealized* caretaker (the idealized selfobject) of infancy and childhood is of course invested by the self of the child with charisma, so that the ministrations of this exalted one—the commands and codes, as well as the soothings—are experienced as divine. The ministrations change over time from the idealized caretaker's expression of soothing to commands which are issued to enforce restraints. However, the ministrations are always experienced as coming from an exalted figure, and therefore are always responded to with alacrity and/or with strong negative feelings.

From the available data, Sam Ealy's parenting in the early part of Lyndon's life consisted in his portraying himself as a model of a powerful persona for young Lyndon. We have no data that reveal him as a calmer or soother who would walk the floors holding a needy youngster. There are several vignettes of his behavior with his son, each of which demonstrate his dissatisfaction with the degree of Lyndon's masculine assertiveness. He was critical of Lyndon's inhibitions against shooting and killing animals (Caro, 1983; Kearns, 1976). He was critical of his son's performances in school and elsewhere (Caro, 1983). He especially did not accept any sign of laziness. It was Sam Ealy who took LBJ at age four to the barbershop to have his curls cut.

The data we have of Johnson's experiences of his father are that he was a free-wheeling and loud presence with whom his mother quarreled frequently and intensely (Kearns, 1976). We know from other descriptions by the various biographers that he was a striking and imposing figure—a handsome, tall cowboy complete with the accoutrements of the Western man which included the Stetson and the six-shooter. His voice was booming, his manner that of the company commander, ordering and expecting obedience. "Straight as a shingle" was a familiar description of him in the State Senate, indicating that he was not for sale to the lobbyists of the oil and gas industry or others (Caro, 1983; Kearns, 1976).

What Lyndon saw as a youngster was a giant who boomed commands and opinions and who camped out often on the front porch with cronies and bourbon and talked of "man things"—such as politics, war, and military campaigns. As Johnson told Doris Kearns that when he was four and running-to-be-caught, one day when they found him and brought him home that *this* time they "sounded good together." Johnson was aware, as he told Kearns, that his mother considered his father's life "vulgar and ignorant. His idea of pleasure was to sit up half the night with his friends, drinking beer, telling stories, and playing dominos" (p. 22).

Johnson's experience of his father was indeed complex and went through many ups and downs. To Doris Kearns (1976) he remarked that his best friend as a boy was his grandfather, whom he talked to each day for two hours or more. This exclusive attention from the patriarch of the family offered, as Johnson said, "the perfect escape from my problems at home" (p. 28). The elder Sam Ealy Johnson had been a genuine cowboy and had been involved in and spoke with relish of Indian attacks, cattle stampedes, and driving herds hundred of miles with bands of cowboys. His grandfather had endless stories to tell which evoked in the boy fantasies in which Johnson became the powerful master cowboy busting up stampedes and thereby overcoming any and all evidence of weakness. Lyndon would take his dog Begam Young to Grandpa Sam Johnson's place, read a story, and be rewarded with a piece of fruit from Grandpa's desk.

When he was five years old, this relationship ended for Lyndon when his family moved to Johnson City. Grandfather Johnson died soon after, and it was then that Johnson turned to his father more intensively as a model to emulate. His imitation of his father extended to the swagger modeled after Sam's gait, and his speech became punctuated with his father's expletives. The gregariousness associated with his father was also mimicked by Lyndon and the overall rowdyism he associated with his father's manner with men, especially when drinking.

In fact, this transformed self stamped Lyndon as a

troublemaker at school, evoking frequent punishment, especially since his distractibility in performing school tasks such as reading now became apparent (it was to become a lifetime source of difficulty). The conflict of values between his mother's standards for learning and refinement and his father's version of life as adventures to be mastered intensified when, at age seven, Lyndon dismissed his mother's attempts to push him into violin and dancing lessons. Three years earlier Lyndon still sported (at four) a full head of curls and wore dresses (Kearns, 1976). Rebekah's reactions to his rejection of the dancing classes with Miss Gidden and the violin lessons with Miss Brodie was to withdraw her interest in Lyndon (Steinberg, 1980). She pretended "I was dead" (Kearns, 1976, p. 25). She would slip into this dismissal of him whenever he did not follow her wishes, as she did when he later refused to go to college.

Indeed, Johnson was a great disappointment to his mother very early in his academic life. It started after the first year of elementary school. There were reports of his inability to sit in class at that time and to be able to learn with the others. His teachers began giving him extra assignments—scut work—as punishment to keep him involved (Kearns, 1976; Steinberg, 1968), not being aware of his difficulty in self-calming. His mother devised a scheme of breakfast-tutoring in which she would discuss his assignments over breakfast since her firstborn son would not—in her view—do his homework (Caro, 1983; Steinberg, 1968). Johnson could never sit easily in class, he did not read as a leisure activity, nor did he ever experience books as sources of pleasure. Books and school never elicited experiences of pleasure, comfort, or were even experienced as a safe activity.

It was during this time—from his fifth to his eleventh year—of attempting to emulate father, that Lyndon listened enthralled to the men of the community and his father in their evening discussions of local and national politics and political heroes such as Teddy Roosevelt, who was always pictured to Lyndon charging on a white horse. When he went around town during these years, Lyndon's swagger and braggadocio became well known. He would, it is recalled by a town resident, appropriate the mailed afternoon paper as soon as it arrived and sit in the barbership in a barber chair and recite the important events from the paper without being invited, even entering into arguments with the men present (Caro, 1983).

Sam Houston Johnson (1969) noted in his biography of his older brother how Sam saw himself drawn to spending as much time as he could with their father, including crack-of-dawn breakfasts, while Lyndon was not. Sam Houston reported of his brother and father's interactions: "There was a kind of tension between them. Even in small unimportant matters they seemed to be competing" (SHJ, 1969, p. 25). As we described earlier, Sam Ealy was often critical of Lyndon. Standing in the kitchen Sam Ealy would say to his wife, "*Your* son Lyndon isn't worth a damn, Rebekah! He'll never amount to a goddamned thing!" (Caro, 1983, p. 102).

LBJ's relations with his father always contained these two elements: the wish to follow his lead and be like him, and the desire to outdo, outdistance, and outsmart him. Even prior to his later disappointments in his father, there were these negative interactions which we have described that did not permit LBJ to enter into a relationship with his father to derive from him what he needed in the way of calming and direction.

One episode that is quoted frequently by the Johnson biographers comes from one of his brother Sam's remembrances of the tension of competition between Lyndon and his father over the leadership within the family. Sam Houston Johnson remembers that when he was three and his brother nine, there was open competition for his services as a bed warmer. On cold winter nights, apparently when mother, Rebekah, was ill or recovering from illness or pregnancy, his father would use him as a body-warmer. He would hear his father call: "Sam Houston, come in here and get me warm." The boy crawled out of the bed he was in, snuggled warmly against his brother, and went to his father's room holding him still until the father fell asleep. Then he would hear Lyndon call, "Sam Houston, come on back, I'm getting cold." He pulled himself out of the father's bed, quietly like a cat-burglar and once again went to his bed to snuggle up to his big brother (Sam Johnson, 1947).

When Johnson was ten, his father began taking him to legislative sessions in Austin, apparently on a regular basis. His father was a special figure in the Texas legislature. He had fought in 1918 to protect the rights of German-Americans then under attack by a group who wished to pass legislation depriving them of their civil liberties. He was known as a unique man, above bribery and above doing favors for the oil, gas, and sulfur interests. He was an old-fashioned populist to the end of his days, identified with causes important and at times life-saving to the common man. He championed the cause of securing free seed and feed for poverty-stricken farmers; he passed legislation to force the big cattle houses to pay small ranchers for their stock promptly.

His most notable piece of legislation, the so-called Johnson Blue Sky Law, created a securities division of the railroad commission that would regulate advertising and sale of stock so that the uninformed would not buy everything but the "blue sky" (Caro, 1983). Johnson, in his conversations with his biographer, Doris Kearns, would say of these times:

> I loved going with my father to the legislature. I would sit in the gallery for hours watching all the activity on the floor and then would wander around the halls trying to figure out what was going on. The only thing I loved more was going with him in the car during his campaigns for reelection. We drove in the Model T Ford from farm to farm, up and down the valley, stopping at every door. Christ, sometimes I wished it could go on forever. (Kearns, 1976, pp. 36–37)

ADOLESCENT TRAUMA: LOSS OF AN IDEAL

A major event transpired in Johnson's life in 1919 when he was eleven years old. His father decided to purchase the entire 433-acre Johnson farm, the entire assets of his now-dead parents. He finally sold it in 1922, driven into bankruptcy by the farm's failure. It was to have been a productive cotton farm, but the soil was too thin, the market for cotton had plummeted to an all-time low, and he could not secure enough capital to keep the farm going when the cotton market went sour. The Johnson family, which had for generations been one of the proudest and most prosperous in their district, became overnight a family known for its debts and its ostentatious display of manners and breeding—the laughingstock of the community. Sam continued to strut for awhile, Rebekah continued to insist that her children were the finest, and Lyndon continued to brag, but everyone in town knew that they were bankrupt and that Sam owed everyone (Caro, 1983).

Thus, when Lyndon was eleven, his family went from the most respected, even idealized group to one to be shunned for their now ridiculous-appearing airs and displays of refinement and hill-country aristocracy (Caro, 1983). Johnson's father, the once-proud legislator, real estate entrepreneur, and farmer, was now humbled into petitioning for work on state construction jobs. He owed money not just to everyone in his town, but in many surrounding towns, wherever he went, cash payments were demanded. His house in Johnson City was mortgaged and he could not keep up with the payments, relying on financial support from his two brothers to keep his family together.

The greatest impact, however, was on his self-esteem. It was clear to all that the tall, robust cowboy was gone, to be replaced by a man who, in his mid-forties, had become old. In fact, shortly after the sale of the farm in 1922, Sam took to his bed for several months with an illness variously designated as "nervous exhaustion" or "pneumonia," and to all observers he seemed gaunt and fragile (Sam Houston Johnson, 1969). According to sources interviewed by Caro, many of the visitors to Sam Johnson during his illness brought food, since it was common knowledge that there was nothing to eat in the house and no money with which to buy any. Sam's previously short-lived episodic temper tantrums now had become more frequent and intensive (Caro, 1983; Cormier, 1977; Dugger, 1982).

The family's financial and social status collapse had several ramifications for Rebekah. After the farm was sold and they moved once again to Johnson City, she was without any domestic help on which she had always relied for cooking, housekeeping, and managing the children. Without her mother and various domestics, neighbors, and relatives, the family could not function properly. Several observers of the Johnsons at this time reported that the family appeared totally disorganized. Dirty dishes piled up, children and clothes went unwashed, and the children went without enough to eat (Caro, 1983).

The impact on Lyndon of the family's social and financial collapse was striking. As Caro reported (1983), based on interviews with relatives and townspeople:

> Lyndon Johnson had been so close to his parents—imitating his father, dressing like him, talking with him, politicking with him, listening to his mother's stories, learning his alphabet and his spelling at her knee, choosing as his favorite poem "I'd Rather Be Mama's Boy." Now his father was still a father who went off to the Legislature and fought for "The People" and wouldn't take any favors from the "the interests," but he was also a father who was the laughingstock of the county. His mother still read poetry and told her children that "principles" were the important thing, and that "a lie is an abomination to the Lord," but she was also a mother that didn't iron, so that he often had to go out in rumpled clothes, and who didn't cook, so that sometimes he went to bed hungry. (p. 99)

The boy who had at least imitated his father at times up to 1922 was a transformed figure after this date, perhaps in conjunction with the failure of the father as a highly respected and adulated figure in his community. His behavior in his teens was marked by attitudes in keeping with a rebel with a cause, the cause being to be against what both mother and father valued. He drank and swore, he was a school truant and when he went to school, did not obey his teachers or keep up with his studies (Kearns, 1976). Now he disobeyed his father's every command: he took the family car at night against his father's wishes, he openly defied him in discussions by challenging his authority, he routinely refused to do the chores assigned to him, and he deliberately outwitted his father by squandering the family funds that had become so precious.

But Johnson would not give in to his father's threats and rage (Johnson's father did spank him frequently), nor to his mother's tears, which were her way of gaining his attention and getting him to conform to her wishes that he abandon his rebellious ways. He continued throughout his adolescence as a rowdy and adventurous youngster always exhibiting his rebelliousness by talking loud, drinking, and driving dangerously. He wrecked the family car twice: on one occasion provoking an eruption of rage in the father, and on the other the following scenario:

> When he was fifteen, Johnson smashed up his father's car. He had borrowed the car to meet a new girl at a church gathering. On meeting Johnson, the girl realized she was three years older and very quickly took off with someone else. Feeling sorry for himself, Johnson gathered a few of his friends and they went off together for a couple of drinks. Then they all piled into the car to go home. On the way, the car hit a bridge and turned upside down. The boys were not hurt, but the car was totally wrecked. Johnson was, as he remembered it, too frightened to know what to do. "I knew only that I could not face my father. I had four dollars in my pocket, so I hopped the bus to New Braunfels, where my uncle lived." I thought I could hide out there for a few days. The second day, Daddy tracked me down on the phone. I walked to the phone, feeling like I was going to the guillotine. I tried to keep my legs and my voice from shaking. My uncle looked at me in silence and I felt the blood rising to my face.
>
> My daddy said: "Lyndon, I traded in the old car of ours this morning for a brand-new one and it's in the store right now needing someone to pick it up. I can't get away from here and I was wondering if you could come back, pick it up, and drive it home for me. And there's one other thing I want you to do for me. I want you to drive it around the courthouse square, five

times, ten times, fifty times, nice and slow. You see there's
some talk around town this morning that my son's a coward,
that he couldn't face up to what he'd done, and that he ran
away from home. Now I don't want anyone thinking I produced a yellow son. So I want you to show up here in that car
and show everyone how much courage you've really got. Do
you hear me?"

"Yes sir," I replied. I hung up the phone, shook hands
with my uncle, and left right away. (Kearns, 1976, p. 38)

At the end of high school, Johnson's career as a
teenage rebel was expected to come to an end. In his
parents' vision he was to go on to college and become an
educated man and go forward in life, not as a working-
man, but as a member of the educated minority who
need not work with their hands—values that were important to his parents. Lyndon informed his parents
that he would not go to college, evoking hours of angry
and sometimes frantic confrontation with Rebekah and
Sam; Rebekah to give way to tears, Sam to rage at him,
but both ineffective in changing Lyndon's mind (Caro,
1983). He actually resisted going on to college for another four years, during which time he went to lengths
difficult to understand. Johnson took a job at backbreaking road gang work, labor that was brutal for all
the other teenagers as well, for two dollars a day. In spite
of his size, Johnson was not strong, not physically coor-
dinated, and not accustomed to physical work.

Johnson continued to engage in daily painful long
harangues with his father and mother over going to college, tolerating his mother's combination of rejections
and dismissals and his father's insults. Rather than go to
college, he literally ran to California to work for a year as
a law clerk with his mother's cousin, Tom Martin. The
year in California was a hectic one since it involved

working with an erratic, alcoholic, and unstable man who often took off for lengthy visits with his mistress.

On his return from California, penniless and gaunt, Johnson again refused to go to college and worked with the road gang for another two years. No data from any of the biographers inform us as to his self-experiences at this time in his life. Johnson did tell Doris Kearns of a repeated dream during this period which we may take as evidence of the young man's feeling abandoned and unable to secure any empathically derived succor. His parents, while continuing to exhort him to go on to college, could not recognize the intensity of the resistance he experienced over exposing himself to college which emerged in this dream:

> In this stormy period, Johnson suffered a recurrent dream that he was sitting alone in a small cage. The cage was completely bare, he said, except for a stone bench and a pile of dark, heavy books. As he bent down to pick up the books, an old lady with a mirror in her hand walked in front of the cage. He caught a glimpse of himself in the mirror and to his horror he found that the boy of fifteen had suddenly become a twisted old man with long, tangled hair and speckled, brown skin. He pleaded with the old woman to let him out, but she turned her head and walked away. At this point in the dream, as he remembered it, he woke up, his hands and his forehead damp and dripping with sweat. He sat up in the bed and then, not fully knowing what he meant by it but believing in it faithfully, he said half aloud: "I must get away." (p. 40)

The association of books and knowledge with imprisonment and the decaying boy makes it clear that to Johnson, school was as fearsome as it had always been. In the dream he was alone and ineffectual with the dread of passivity and surrender to the woman, who was to him, as always, the purveyor of life and of possible abandonment.

Characteristically, Johnson ended this four-year period of staving off the fearful inevitability of leaving his
mother—once again to others—and the old ties with her
by enlisting her aid. He actually took her with him to
the college at San Marcos since she "had" to come to
help him pass the entrance examinations.

For Johnson who started running-to-get-caught by
his mother so early in life, total separation from his
mother by entering college apparently was a prospect
too frightening to be entertained. As we have seen, he
always managed to keep her involved with him through
being "in trouble." She was forced to devote breakfast
time to his school deficiencies throughout elementary
school; he kept her reminded of his needs through
school failures and truancies throughout high school.
While his father Sam's reactions to his reenactment of
ineptitude was to criticize him directly ("everyone in
town is up while you're still sleeping") or through depreciating him to Rebekah, Rebekah's response was to
exhort him to perform better and, from time to time,
dismiss him.

And when he was finally about to leave her to enter
college—a step he had avoided for four years—the anxiety released in him compelled him to a perfect solution:
Rebekah would come with him. Entering college was, in
our view, experienced as a major separation from the
source of narcissistic supplies (as witness the letters of
entreaty he wrote her throughout his college days). College represented the growth away from home that he
had resisted for so long. To a man who had experienced
maternal deprivation and continued to enter into archaic
ties with his mother to drag out these supplies, the sep-

aration in entering into the next phase of his life was a threat to his self-life.

At the close of his teenage years we can now describe the self of Johnson as his characteristic or modal self. This is the finished person, in essence, which changed over time only in terms of the projects in which he was embroiled or attempting to master, or the people from whom he was attempting to gain self-supplies. The essential features of this self, crystallized at the end of adolescence, were all centered, it is surmised here, on his striving to maintain his self-esteem so as never to be vulnerable to rebuff, or to losing. He tried to remain the dominant figure in the ball game or in the debate or in a drinking bout by choosing the social activity for the night or the comrades whom he could dominate. And if the project or activity was unsuccessful—such as the year he spent in California as legal assistant to his cousin, Tom Martin—Lyndon would glamorize it or present it in a manner that demonstrated his cunning.

His lack of respect for veracity was well known from his childhood. The name of his game was always to preserve his self-regard and never appear inept in any activity or in any relationship.

It is fundamental to grasp this central aspect of Johnson's self—the unremitting drive toward self-protection against any suggestion of inferiority. At any cost to *anyone,* his self had, from childhood, to be protected against what was to him the terrifying possibility of presenting a self-state of inadequacy.

As we will describe more fully in later chapters, Johnson's need for applause and direction were accompanied by the fear of being unsuccessful in obtaining these supplies of worth and calming, and thus being needy was equated in his mind with the pain of failure. Although in his interactions with people he clamored for attention, he would never admit that these needs for attention reflected an underlying state of inferiority. Indeed, the state of inferiority was unconsciously shunted away from the rest of his self. These two phenomena—the actions he took to acquire attention, the clamoring self—and the underlying state of inferiority which propelled the clamoring were kept separate in Johnson's psyche through the phenomenon called disavowal. Disavowal is an unconscious defense mechanism which Johnson utilized to separate his inferiority from the rest of his psyche. Thus while he clamored for recognition from everyone in his field of vision, he unconsciously repudiated the meaning of his clamoring behaviors, namely that his self-regard and self-calming functions were inadequate to maintain a cohesive psyche. In short, his state of need was never communicated directly, the statement "I feel needy" was never expressed. The *behaviors* of demanding interest—without revealing the underlying need—by jumping to center stage and staying there was what Johnson did. So often in his life, Johnson—as a student, as a congressman, as a vice president and certainly as a president—hid his defects and his difficulties. He could never admit to anyone that he was wrong in any matter.

However, with all his attempts to maintain the cohesive self, it is important to note that the face-saving efforts were never wholly successful. Through his entire lifetime, as we will see, Lyndon Johnson always experienced emptiness, loneliness, a fear of loss of self-worth, agitation (his so-called great source of energy), intense

vulnerability to rebuff or loss, rage attacks, and fragmentation states.

Lyndon Johnson came out of his years with his
caretakers short on the self-supplies that are needed for
intrapsychic peace. As he told his biographer, Doris
Kearns (1976), "I was always very lonely" (p. 70). We
know that his mother failed him in his need for adequate
mirroring, as witness his unending insatiable insistence
on extracting from everyone he met their vital juices,
which never appeased the strivings of the unfed infant
and youngster. The selfobject deprivations of the mirroring functions and the functions of the calming selfobject fueled, we surmise, the hyperkinetic youngster on
the make since infancy, running away to derive some
soothing and structure. Many in his environment saw
only the defensive attempts, especially the defensive
grandiosity with which he attempted to get applause,
the supplies of worth from whoever he met.

Rebekah's other empathic failures were in the absence of her mirroring of his adaptive behaviors at age
seven and thereafter. Approbation for his horsemanship
or his farming skills would have been empathic to
young Lyndon rather than attempting to create a violinist or dancer. She could not empathize with his obvious
difficulties in learning and berated him or closed him off
from her rather than acknowledge the manifest fears he
revealed of going to college.

From the men in his background, Lyndon could not
derive the compensatory narcissistic supplies that were
required to ensure in him the genuine experience of
adequate self-regard, rather than the obvious attempts
to irrationally proclaim his imaginary power through
his various and obvious attempts at defensive grandi-

osity. No one could miss his braggadocio, by which he was simply trying to overcome painful states of inadequacy from which he was in lifelong terror. Not to be recognized was a dread to him up to his death as well as in his developing years.

The idealization process may be interfered with in several ways: the unavailability of the identified selfobject through separations, the failure of the selfobject to perform as a valued or important person, the hostility of the selfobject toward the self wishing to merge. In all these instances, the self, deprived of the structures necessary for the formation of a cohesive self, develops a lifelong hunger to form contact with an idealizable figure who can be a leader. The pathognomonic feature of these contacts is that the ideal-hungry self, attempting to establish an *archaic* self/selfobject dyad, is doomed to disappointment. For the *archaic* needs for a selfobject, the wish to be given *total* direction can never be gratified in adult life.

One final area of breakdown of this process is the idealizing shortfall that occurs due to a previous massive failure in mirroring from the primary source of esteem. This then hypertrophies the need for secondary esteem-building through forming a compensatory idealized self/selfobject dyad. In these situations of intense mirroring failures, the fixation that occurs (the so-called lifelong mirror-hungry person) perhaps never allows for *any* compensation through the formation of an idealized parent bond.

Thus Johnson experienced a failure from both primary and secondary sources of self-esteem, a condition that tragically ensures a lifetime of selfobject-seeking that never can be satisfied.

SUMMARY REMARKS

What characterizes the response to our query at the beginning of this chapter: Where does it come from? Is it that Lyndon Johnson was a youngster whose life was permanently handicapped by the unique deprivations to which he was subjected? We will first direct our enquiry to the successes and failures of his encounters with his mother and then to the successes and failures with his other major selfobject influences in childhood.

The documents and the direct interviews with Johnson related to his mother point to an involvement on her part centered on his intellectual growth and achievement; *and* an equally important absence of involvement in other areas of development for the adaptive needs of a youth in the culture and community in Southeastern Texas. Other areas of her functioning are less clear from all the available documents such as her everyday capacity to show warmth through the tissue contacts of embraces, kissing, and rocking. He apparently saw little in the way of affection between Rebekah and Sam Ealy from the accumulated data. She did demonstrate protectiveness, perhaps even overconcern for Lyndon's safety from the river and the wildlife in the area. The way in which she showed concern was either to cry and become agitated or to freeze Lyndon out of her world, the "Johnson freeze-out," as others would refer to it on his own part. Her insistence that her son was perfect impelled her to gloss over his disruptiveness, as Johnson's aide and biographer Booth Mooney discovered, when she read his first biography on Johnson (Mooney, 1966). She disputed any episode that portrayed her son in any way that was even slightly negative.

Rebekah Johnson's own volume of remembrances of the family shows Lyndon in an unrecognizably idealized light, with no mention of the disruptive behaviors in speech and manner for which he was known even as a youngster (RBJ, 1960). She continued in her idealizing and therefore unempathic mission to sculpt a Lord Lyndon out of the boy, offering violin lessons, now giving him dancing lessons. She imposed her own cultural and intellectual values on him to mold her own idealized hero, with no recognition of the other influences on Lyndon, or of her own financial limitations to subsidize an artist in any case. Besides, Rebekah Johnson had four other children and a husband with the needs for a caretaker and a wife, also limiting her mission to groom the idealized scion of her fantasies (Kearns, 1976; Caro, 1983).

The mirroring that Johnson received from Rebekah Baines was *selective,* as we have seen. Rebekah's program of action for Lyndon was designed to construct a hero programmed with her values. If Lyndon stayed in curls, he was mirrored. If Lyndon recited well, he was mirrored and violently embraced. Conversely, if he demonstrated behaviors more modal for his milieu—a boy surrounded by animals, guns, and other symbols of the cowboy—he was bereft of mirroring and subjected to the "freeze-out."

Another source of selfobject deprivations is highlighted not by direct observations but by accumulated observations and by the behavior which we can surmise to have resulted. This is that Rebekah withdrew herself in large part from her oldest son when he was three, and from then on was inconsistently involved in his emotional and intellectual needs, a shadow of the caretaker she had been until he was three years of age when the two of them had been a unit.

Observers agree that Rebekah Baines was not a competent housekeeper, given the size of her family and for the rigors of conditions in that part of the United States in the early 1900s. After Lyndon was two, and every two years thereafter until he was eight years of age, Rebekah was pregnant. Each pregnancy was followed by an increase in her maternal responsibilities but not by an enhancement of her capabilities as a caretaker of the young. Lyndon was, it seems, subject to a dramatic transformation in the caretaking he had received from his infancy and thereafter. While Rebekah continued throughout her life, as we have described, to urge Lyndon into the program to which she was committed, she could not be available in the same way after his infancy.

Not only must she feed, hold, and change a new baby, and launder and cook for the family, she was expected to be a wife as well. Another source of deprivation, perhaps the major one, is suggested in the report that Rebekah Baines became withdrawn as the responsibilities of mothering became overwhelming to her. Now for periods of time she was totally unavailable to Lyndon and everyone as she retreated to her bed and into her inner life.

As will be recalled from the earlier descriptions of Lyndon as a child, he began his hiding and running-to-be-caught before he was three. Sometime early in his childhood and certainly by four years of age, his tactics became sufficiently polished to gain recognition from his caretakers. His exploits were calculated, we could say, to structure a responsive surround.

Of course, deprivation does not of itself ensure that fixation of the self will result. The compulsive behavior of the fixated self, striving to duplicate the actual experiences of the past ultimately to derive the held-out gratification, is a multifactorial event. Several variables are involved. One variable is the *intensity* of the deprivation. This was certainly keen in Johnson's life. Another important variable in fixation comprises constitutional factors: the plasticity of the central nervous system; the ability of the nervous system to form new circuits. The other variables involved are the presence or absence of a surrogate selfobject, or the presence of a compensatory selfobject.

Another strong source of support for those whose primary source of esteem is deficient or missing is a caretaker who can perform similar functions as the original but flawed selfobject. In Johnson's case there was no surrogate selfobject. This is often the case in a large nuclear family. No older sisters, aunts, or grandmothers were available on a regular basis to become invested with caretaking features by Lyndon. Thus there were no surrogate selfobjects in his interpersonal world who could fill the void in infancy and childhood, so as to avert the compulsive seeking of the lost selfobject of infancy. This then became the quest of his entire life, but with the added feature of the everpresent fear of exposure of his hidden (disavowed) self-of-inferiority.

The selfobject functions offered for internalization by the caretakers in the realm of the idealized parent operations are, it is to be hoped, provided for in each developing self. But in the development of a self that has been provided less-than-optimal mirroring, the requirements of the idealized selfobject now differ. In these situations, when there has been a deficit in the primary caretaker's operations—the mirroring selfobject functions and with them the self internalization of these functions—a compensatory selfobject is crucial for the fate of the self. Since Johnson's lack of success with his primary provider, his mirroring maternal selfobject, his requirement of self-supplies from those who could be his surrogate and/or compensatory selfobject was not just to add to a large store of interiorized self-worth. It was to make up the deficits, a difficult task.

Sam Ealy was always "around" the house; though he was away at times as a member of the Texas legislature, and selling and buying real estate, his presence was always palpable. His swagger, his booming voice, his freely expressed opinions, his cowboy garb, his use of invective, and his repertoire of racy stories when drinking with buddies were part of Lyndon's childhood experiences of his father. Merging with these images and functions of an authority figure so as to internalize his strength was available to Lyndon, and as observers attested, he walked, talked, cursed, grabbed lapels and "hollered," bragged, and drank very much as his father did. Mimicry, however, is not reflective of the process of internalization of an idealized parent whose leadership functions are empathically attuned to the younger and can be easily acquired. Johnson's father was always described at all ages and stages of Lyndon's childhood and adolescent development as so critical of his eldest son that an ongoing relationship of love could not be effected. Sam Ealy never really rejected his son. He showed concern for his Lyndon's welfare, educational and career plans. But it was never enough. We possess no record of the thousands of instances of interactions that could give us the behavioral data of the relationship between Lyndon and Sam Ealy. But even if more behavioral material were available, it could not provide us with the data of the experiential—what Johnson did ultimately take in of his father's leadership. Was Johnson calmed in his contacts with this father? What of the sufficiency of the father's teachings? What of the father's political and social advice were evident in Johnson's self? Did his father's infusion of vigor correct for any part of Johnson's needs for esteem?

To all these queries, the data reveal that for Johnson his father was not the idealized parent who shored up a enfeebled self. This assertion should quickly be followed by the comment that the deprivation in Johnson's life might never have been able to be altered by *any* compensatory selfobject. Lyndon's father, or any father, might never have been able to infuse him with enough worth or vigor to overcome the *original* deprivation wrought in the early days of his interactions with his mother. It certainly was true, as all have observed, that Johnson almost frantically sought out and engaged an army of "political daddies" to guide him; but these choices shifted in swift succession, and as with Gandhi, while continuing in the endless search for a guru, the throne always remained vacant (Muslin & Desai, 1985).

In psychoanalytic therapy we measure the success of the treatment by the degrees of freedom from their past that our patients attain. The development of the modal self we measure by the degree of internalization that has been achieved: how much of the selfobject's teaching, or calming, or firmness, or approval has been interiorized.

Measured by this scale Lyndon Johnson's developmental achievements in the area of acquired self-worth were modest. His developmental achievements in the areas of self-calming and the interiorization of the precepts of his parents also were limited. As we have now set forth, Johnson was deficient and therefore seeking in the two major areas of self-life: He needed and clamored for *recognition*, often resembling the hungry infant; he needed and clamored for *direction* from an all-powerful and calming leader, albeit throughout his life he never exposed to *anyone* that he experienced himself as defective in any manner. These two major strivings, in addition to a value system that was markedly at odds with his proper mother's and his high-minded straight-as-a-shingle father's, point also to the failures in his development. The processes of child/parent, self/selfobject merging ideally are followed by the transmuting internalizations that transform an unformed, seeking child to a robust, joyous self with parental standards now firmly internalized to live by, an endogenous pool of self-love and self-soothing.

We can summarize these findings by stressing that the self of Lyndon Johnson was not sufficiently nurtured through the selfobject activities of his caretakers. This resulted in the perpetuation throughout his life of longings and strivings which are particulars of the infant and childhood self, both in the nature of the strivings and the psychomotor behaviors. Lyndon Johnson was not merely filled with unexposed needs for recognition; his behaviors, verbal and nonverbal, were those of the clamoring youngster striving to achieve a measure of well-being always from his surround since he was without adequate endogenous sources of worth and calming.

It can now be said that we have gathered sufficient data in response to our second research query, "Where does it come from?" We can say with some surety that Johnson's intrapsychic life was filled, albeit unconsciously, with wishes to extract from all those around him the gratifications he missed from his caretakers.

In the next chapter, we will describe Johnson's entry into college at San Marcos and then into the world of politics in Washington.

Chapter 5

THE COMPLETED TRAGIC SELF OF LYNDON B. JOHNSON

This chapter discusses the completed self of Lyndon Johnson. It *is* a tragic self—the term denoting those who are constantly haunted by a sense of pervasive emptiness. These are people whose thirst for recognition can never be appeased in present interactions. Their needs could be gratified only by a reemergence of the buried relationships of childhood which might, this time around, result in a positive outcome—to finally gain a measure of approval or direction. Those who possess a tragic self feel a loneliness that is not reduced by the company of other people in their adult life nor by any joyous events of the day. At most they may feel a momentary uplift in mood and from the victory over failure—the avoidance of inferiority although their inner experience may be at great variance with their outward behaviors of frenzied ebullience or grandiosity.

Johnson's completed self showed other aspects of

those who suffer with narcissistic (self-worth) deficits. He carried with him throughout his life hypersensitivity to any measure of rebuff. His basic fear was that revealing ineptitude might usher in the dreaded aloneness, the reduplication of the withdrawal of "mirroring," or the reduplicated loss of a caretaker selfobject. He suffered "attacks" of loss-of-worth in reaction to disappointments or failures even as vice president or president since again it ushered in the dreaded self of inferiority. During these attacks he became immobilized.

Throughout his life he was hyperkinetic. The "Johnson trot," the "Johnson hustle," all these descriptions from his observers make it clear that Johnson had what we have called sparse endogenous supplies of self-calming (Evans & Novak, 1973; SHJ, 1969).

The usual plight of those who have narcissistic (self-worth) deficits is that their object world is a *selfobject* (caretaker) world, rather than the real, here-and-now world. They unconsciously structure their interactions with significant persons so that the significant other is imbued with the role of a caretaker (an "archaic selfobject"). They experience themselves in a *regressive* mode. This is the revived-infantile-self seeking its primary caretakers in order to gain narcissistic (self-worth) supplies (Kohut, 1971, 1977). The experienced archaic selfobject may be an individual or an institution. Thus, the American public may be telescoped into *one* entity which may be a source of encouragement, or may be dismissive.

Another manifestation of the narcissistic deficit in Johnson was his vulnerability to fragmentation of his self. This is the outcome of a breakup between the self and its caretakers (selfobjects). In those whose relatedness to others is marked by seeking people out to unconsciously "be" a selfobject, the breakup of these relationships (archaic dyads) often ushers in a massive (disintegration) anxiety. A so-called fragmentation reaction ensues, with loss of cohesiveness of the self and periods of weakened reality testing and judgment.

At times this fragmentation reaction leads to a rageful, regressive self-state in which there is no "target" for the egress of its rage. Anyone and everyone around may be the victim of the outpouring of venom. The stimulus for the rage was not a particular person. It was the experience of a precipitous break between the self and its source of worth—a self/selfobject rupture—evoked by a current disappointment or rebuff: thus the designation, narcissistic rage.

In this summary of the self-states that he presented, it is important again to mention that Johnson, although he appeared to be deeply involved in human encounters, was always guarded, as if to be sure that no one "owned" him. Whether it was a ball game or the communal donkey, or Lady Bird, Johnson was in charge and in control so that no one possessed him, and therefore no one could abandon him. The price he paid for these defenses against opening up to anyone was the sense of loneliness, the direct result of his inability, out of dread of desertion, to give himself completely to a human bond to gain the solace ("succor") of a merger with a caretaker.

And so the completed self of Johnson was one needy of the archaic selfobject functions; at the same time showing two self-fixtures that militated against his ever gaining intrapsychic comfort. One was the defense of aloofness, as described, the defense against admitting supplies of mirroring and "calming" into one's self. The other was the necessity always to control his environment so that he could never be abandoned. His need for company or other human supports could only emerge in clamoring through spasmodic petitions for love, and then, just as suddenly, pulling back, because he feared criticism and/or dismissal.

He did make superficial contact with people easily, unlike his predecessor JFK. His self-supplies of worth being limited, he reached out to a large body of experts and other partial selfobjects. But this was always in the style of *vigilant* unfolding. He was always primed to pull out if necessary to avoid painful desertion or disillusionment.

We now turn from the profile of the completed tragic self of Johnson to discussion of the processes that maintained Johnson's completed self. We are at the final inquiry into his psyche: What *functions* are *served* by this tragic self? Put another way, what psychological gratifications, conscious and unconscious, are afforded by this self? In clinical practice, the analyst or therapist tracking down a symptom or a self/selfobject interaction ultimately asks the patient: "What is this archaic self/ selfobject interaction *doing* in the here-and-now? Of what value is this ancient self to you *today?*"

These questions epitomize the challenge in the psychotherapy or the psychoanalysis to illuminate the *fixation* in a person's development—the piece of the past in the present—and then to extricate the patient from these archaic ties, so that he/she may live in the here-and-now in safety—that is, without fears of criticism or rejection. Fixation refers to the limitation in development due to a confluence of forces, especially deprivation by the mirroring and/or idealized parent selfobject. Apart from cases of extended and intense deprivation, the process of fixation usually involves both the absence of an adequate surrogate selfobject, and inadequate compensatory selfobject. The compensatory selfobject is usually the idealized parent, whose function is to build up esteem in a person who has had inadequate involvement with a mirroring selfobject, the primary source of esteem (cf. Chapter 1). Apart from these psychological variables, the central nervous system is always involved in a fixation process. People vary a great deal in their capacity to construct neuronal circuits and therefore also in moving away from a fixation on their archaic selfobjects by forming new circuits.

The fixation process refers to the repetitious seeking of the actual childhood caretaker. In this attempt to reenact and relive events from the past, especially the self/selfobject transferences, the unconscious hope is to reclaim the missing selfobject gratifications of mirroring and/or calming. The person caught in an unconscious fixation of an archaic self/selfobject world unconsciously reenacts old ways of obtaining selfobject gratifications. This entails rejecting the current world of gratifications, with its mature objects and mature selfobjects. Each of Lyndon Johnson's fixations was an obvious attempt to recreate and relive the archaic mirroring scenes, as well as to search out and bond with an archaic idealized selfobject, although these relationships were always transitory, due to his fears of total bonding.

An important aspect of the reenactment process is the reenactment of the defense transference, an archaic selfobject toward whom one maintains a defensive, removed position and whom one does *not* openly petition for supplies. This defensive posture is based on a fear of the reexperienced rejection by the disappointing or hateful archaic selfobject.

Another important aspect of the fixation process which fuels the reenactment of the past is the tendency to turn away from the here-to-now world of bonding and mature gratifications and hark back to the archaic world. When patient and therapist can study those instances in which the patient turns away from his current world of mature gratification, a vital insight is gained. The patient will see that he has entered into another relationship in which he attempts to duplicate the archaic world of being a naif with a goddess or god, the recreated, not necessarily beautiful world of their past.

These instances of fixation are the stuff of psychoanalytic therapy: Again and again the therapist confronts the patient with his reenactments. The patient then becomes aware of the turning to the past for nurturance, as if the Magna Mater of his early days continues to be the only or major purveyor of life. This process, called the "working-through" phase of psychoanalysis, is at the heart of the curative process and, when it is successful, results in a person no longer attaching to his archaic selfobjects for self-life (Muslin, 1986). Those whose object world continues to be dominated in their adult life by reenactments recreate their total archaic world in many or all of their current interactions. They enter into the self they formerly were, and they experience the person with whom they are currently involved as an archaic selfobject.

The life of Lyndon Johnson presents many instances in which his world of the present reflected the world of his past. His interactions with people often were, in his psychic reality, reenactments with people and situations from which he hoped to derive what every person (self) strives for in their reenactments. This is the mirroring, or the direction, or the togetherness that was not forthcoming from their original relationships with their selfobjects.

The two major self strivings of Johnson were (1) the striving for mirroring—the experience of being applauded and approved, which normally ends developmentally in the self-experiences of worth through internalization of the caretaker's admiration (mirroring); and (2) the search to acquire a "guru" to satisfy the need to be calmed and directed. In Lyndon Johnson's life, from the hill country of Texas to the White House and back, his entire world in his experience became an audience to applaud his performances. He would alter his actions in ways designed as performances to provoke the *maximum response* from the audience. Wherever Johnson went throughout his life was a potential audience to give him his required mirroring—a baseball game, a debate, a drinking contest, a contest for editor of a college newspaper, a congressman's constituency, the nation, the world. In each of these arenas he would do whatever was required to be the "best" or "most" or "first" or "worst" or "most rebellious." He demanded and received his share of the available admiration.

In his preschool years, as we have described, he ran, to get caught by anyone or everyone just to receive much-needed responses—in his view—from his family. In grammar school he was special from the beginning, he demanded a certain adaptation on his teacher's part and got it; she would take him on her lap as mother Rebekah did and then he would read for her. Subsequently, in elementary school Johnson enlarged his repertoire of tactics in and out of school to make his environment accommodate to his mirroring needs. He was so charming (or so disruptive) in his classes he made his teachers give him extra chores and thereby extra attention. By making sure his preparation for class was inadequate he made his mother spend time devoted solely to him at the start of each day so as to ensure that he would be prepared. At school, from marbles to baseball, Lyndon had to be "first" or "most." In the community, in his preadolescent days, whether it was advertising, his shoeshine business, or reading the daily newspaper aloud in the barbershop for any audience, Johnson was always "on."

In later years his appetites for mirroring had to undergo a change to fit what was admirable to high school students and accordingly he became a roughneck, a loud-talking, cussing, debauching rebel without a cause. In college again his tactics had to be altered to fit the values of the culture. But the overall strategy, to obtain self-worth supplies, remained constant through his life. Wherever there was an audience he played to it, in order to extract the available mirroring.

In college he developed a new tactic that was to become a major part of his mirror-gathering devices throughout the rest of his life: assuming control. He sought to control institutions and people in order to guarantee the mirroring, the narcissistic supplies he needed. In college he sought and captured the executive presidency and took over the newspaper. He founded a student political organization which, of course, he ran. He developed a cadre of students subservient to him and assumed control over jobs for students.

Later, as a congressman's secretary, he acquired new tactics to adapt to the new surroundings and its requirements for obtaining the applause. He became a totally work-oriented person. From dawn to dusk he labored mightily to impress his boss and the constituents of his boss's district. Evolving from a high school ruffian and lazy scholar to this workaholic young man demonstrated how far Lyndon would go when his imperative need for mirroring was at stake. After he left Rebekah and the family, diminished in endogenous self-worth as he was, his demands of the world were particularly exorbitant.

In Congress and in the Senate the process continued to bespeak the man always in search of the applause. Once again he had to alter his tactics to achieve his goal of being the apple of someone's eye. He had to learn to "polish up" to "Mister Sam" Rayburn and abstain from upstaging the other congressman. These tactics paid off handsomely. Soon Mister Sam, the speaker himself was functioning as a mirroring selfobject. Johnson had already learned the value of being well prepared on any piece of legislation from his work as Kleberg's secretary; also the value of knowing the different agencies and people that would best serve the needs of the district. Johnson received many kudos from "his" constituency for the many requests he was able to fulfill and the projects he started that were of service to the community—the dams, the electrification projects, the public housing, and a great many more.

In his Senate years another set of adaptations had to take place to obtain the needed mirroring. This time he had to become a "Southern" senator and to adjust to other styles of the main dispenser of mirroring, Richard Russell of Georgia. His style of speech and manner became altered to become a member of the Southern reactionary club and again he was successful in making the necessary self-alterations.

While he was a senator his constituency underwent a change, since he now represented the entire state of Texas. To get elected and remain in office in Texas was to become involved in, or at least not antagonistic to, the interests of the barons in the oil, gas, and sulphur industries, and to business tycoons in general. Once FDR died and he became a senator, Johnson again was able to give up his seemingly interiorized values of populism and to work in the interests of the monied members of his constituency. With their backing he financed his first and subsequent campaigns for senator and rapidly became the fair-haired boy of the real estate, oil, and newspaper empires of Texas (Dugger, 1982).

Even prior to his senatorial days he added another weapon to his arsenal toward the acquisition of mirroring—his own financial empire. With the ownership of the radio station in Austin, Johnson began his determined quest to inflate himself into a Texas baron. When he became president, he was the most personally monied of all presidents up to that time, with a private fortune of at least $14 million (Kearns, 1976).

Now came the greatest mirroring opportunity of his life; to be recipient of the country's and the free world's admiration as President of the United States, taking the place of the fallen John Kennedy. His initial burst of energy in the onslaught to capture everyone's acclaim was wondrous to behold: The extent of legislation that was passed in his first session as president was of record proportions. However, tragically for the world and for Johnson, the entry into the Vietnam war and the way in which it was prosecuted left Johnson nationally and globally deprived of support. He went from being celebrated to being despised in a short four years.

As we have noted earlier, we are told by Johnson watchers (Caro, 1983; Kearns, 1976; Steinberg, 1968) that for Johnson the process of going through elections in the best of circumstances evoked a great deal of fear. His fear of dismissal, from childhood on, was all-powerful, and so he suffered physically and mentally at all of his electoral contests. He buckled and required lavish protestations of his worth from Lady Bird to continue his campaign and stand for the election in 1964.

As the Vietnam war raged on in increasing public awareness of its horrors and the mounting toll of American lives, Johnson's supplies of mirroring were being dried up. Not only was the war draining our resources but the nation's economy was in trouble. There was massive social unrest. Beleaguered by these failures, Johnson's self-cohesiveness showed increasing signs of collapse. He revealed more and more intense anxiety to his intimates, centering his attention on different figures whom he invested with hostile or malicious intent toward him and his programs.

These episodes of fragmentation are described by several sources (Goodwin, 1987; Kearns, 1976). They attest to the concept that for Johnson the removal of mirroring was experienced as a relived self/selfobject rupture. Suddenly, memories of the failures of nurturance from his mother were revived. Those disappointments, we can surmise, forced him originally to begin his lifelong search for self supplies. As several observers have documented, Johnson's self-decompensations occurred several times during the latter part of his presidency. Each time, we witness the complete syndrome of fragmentation: anxiety, narcissistic rage with paranoid reactions directed toward different people, Bobby Kennedy the most prominent, whom he thought was "out to get him" (Caro, 1983; Kearns, 1976). These reactions will be elaborated more fully in Chapter 6 on Johnson's self-reactions during the Vietnam war.

To turn to the search for a "guru," Johnson, like his

seeming antithesis, Gandhi, was destined to search endlessly for the "perfect" idealized parent but, like Gandhi, never to be satisfied. Gandhi said, at fifty-seven, after yet another of his disappointments with a potential guru, "And yet in spite of this high regard for him, I could not enthrone him in my heart as my guru. The throne has remained vacant and my search still continues" (Gandhi, 1957, p. XII).

When Lyndon finally became a student at San Marcos, he turned with intensity to capture the self of Cecil Evans, the college president. In making Evans his target for idealization Lyndon hoped to merge with his strength and his values so as to overcome the aloneness evoked by the abandonment of the boy/man Lyndon by his mother. Although he was able to attach himself to Evans, he continued to maintain contact with Rebekah. This pattern of attempting to evoke an experience of merging with an idealized figure while continuing to evoke a selfobject experience from Rebekah—a mixture of mirroring, for being "good" and "performing well" (from Rebekah)—and the selfobject leader functions of getting direction and control ("daddies"), continued through LBJ's life. A sample of this phenomenon is contained in these letters reminding Rebekah that Lyndon was alone:

> "Dearest Mother," he wrote once, "Have all of my books arranged before me in preparation for a long evening of study. You can't realize the difference in atmosphere after one of your sweet letters. I know of nothing so stimulating and inspiring to me as one of your encouraging, beautifully-written letters...Mother I love you so. Don't neglect me...." (Caro, 1983, p. 148)

As an aside, Rebekah wrote to him almost every day and continued to do so until her death 30 years later.

Lyndon, certainly through college, wrote to her several times a week.

The voyage to San Marcos became the psychological passage to Johnson's formed adult self. At the end of his college experience, the standards were set for his lifelong goals, the ambitiousness crystallized to action programs, the skills and talents polished to tactics to realize his goals: the attainment of power and the domination of whatever group he would enter. The corollary lifetime motto became: Never be in the subservient role—which, for Lyndon, was permanently connected to the experience of the ever-feared abandonment once he became subservient. Achievement of these goals by developing skills of leadership over men would avoid the experience of shame through a victory over weakness.

Yet these values have nothing to do with the goals, espoused in action, of his father who was a populist, a hater of the KKK, a fighter for the rights of the common man against the entrenched gas, oil, and sulphur tycoons. Moreover, these values had no part in the gentility and cultural affinities that dominated his mother's outlook. As we have already reported in part, Rebekah dismissed, either through unconscious denial or conscious avoidance, the manifest data of any of her son's wrongdoing or excesses (RBJ, 1965; Mooney, 1964).

And it was also at San Marcos that the tactics LBJ used for a lifetime, his lifelong attempts to gain support for his constantly flagging self-worth by extracting power from leaders, were calculated to perfection. These methods of assuring self-esteem were not the only modes of accruing worth, as we described in previous sections. We will now describe the life-style of power accumulation in detail sufficient to show the ex-

tent of these activities in Johnson and how they dominated his life. The processes by which Johnson acquired
the power from the leaders he plugged into, which
could be likened to a transfusion from the power source
into his antecubital vein, exploded as soon as he left
home. The former lazy adolescent rebel and road gang
laborer metamorphosed into the enterprising student, a
man suddenly infused with a mission. It is clear from
the accounts of these days in his life that a self-transfor-
mation had taken place.

Our surmise is that when he was suddenly cast out
into the world of purposefulness, his anxiety, evoked by
aloneness—connected with going to school as in the
past—stimulated his compensatory tactics of arranging
for power transfusions. The trip to San Marcos, only 40
miles from home, was also the separation from the daily
presence of Rebekah. He of course always attempted to
keep her involved with his new lives wherever he went;
but the separation experience necessitated a transfusion
of power. And so at San Marcos commenced the tactics
of power-acquiring, not value acquiring. The strategies
that he became known for in later years were honed
here. They consisted of subservience when it was indicated or when it worked, availability for any mission at
any time for the identified power broker leader; and
extracting the mana through argumentation and/or duplicity. Power accumulation became a central drive in
Johnson's life; if you had power you had it all, namely
the sources of worth. Then, as for the addict who defends against human sources of worth, no human purveyor of worth was required.

Further, as an addict of power (rather than an as-if
person), Johnson's method of merging to attain the
power was to become temporarily like the person to

whom he was petitioner. After the power grab was made, the other person's values could be discarded. After FDR's death, Johnson was able with no difficulty to become involved in the reactionary politics of Richard Russell. The data that we have gathered reveal that Johnson was not capable of the total merging process that provides for the experience of intrapsychic power and total well-being, i.e., to achieve a self of adequate self-worth. Thus Johnson, attempting to gain compensation for the experience of diminished self-regard, was riveted upon power, getting it, using it, never losing it.

At San Marcos, with the initial target, Carl Evans, Johnson plunged into an apprentice-master relationship, one of his most successful postures to accomplish his power-grabbing mission. President Evans wielded, after all, the primary power at the school, which included distribution of jobs essential for poor students who needed to earn their way. Johnson, along with most, came to college with no cash reserve, and had to work for his tuition, room, and board. Early in his freshman year, Johnson sought out Prexy Evans and began without hesitation to engage him in conversations apparently over a mutually interesting topic, the state politics of Texas. Johnson was quite sophisticated in the political scene in Austin, and Evans, it turned out, was interested in local and national politics. Soon Johnson began to run errands for President Evans and his wife, and then began working for Evans as an office boy, ensconced right outside his office.

As time went on, the president became more attached to this devoted student who would seemingly do anything to accommodate him. Evans took the young Johnson to Austin on his trips to present the budget to the legislature. He gave him a say in assigning students to campus jobs; this of course made Johnson a kingpin at this poor boys' and girls' college.

Johnson's flattery did not stop at Evans. It was at the ready in his approach to all the faculty and, at times, administrative officials and dormitory matrons, depending on what could be accrued from each of them. If a professor held an informal session anywhere on the campus, Johnson would be there sitting at the professor's feet with his face turned up to him, his entire body transfixed in admiration (Caro, 1983).

The power that Johnson absorbed from Evans he utilized in his dealings with the students as he became more and more of a leader. He soon functioned like a college administrator rather than a student. People were surprised when they found that this personable young man was only a student, after the way he greeted people at the front door of the President's office and spoke to them as if he were at least a dean (Caro, 1983).

In each of his subsequent dealings with these avuncular figures, political and otherwise, Johnson demonstrated the tactics he had acquired at San Marcos in the successful transfusion of power. He also had learned the lessons of hard work and attention to detail in any project he entered, and had begun to appreciate his own capacity for comprehension and retention.

His next target for power transfusion was Congressman Richard Kleberg who hired him to go to Washington as his secretary. He "became" the congressman so completely after a relatively short period that people in Kleberg's constituency knew that if you needed a favor in Washington you called Lyndon Johnson. He worked at a feverish pace through the usual daily correspondence and wrote to these constituents using his own hand, so that they got to know him. He thereby developed a list of people from whom he could ask favors in the future in Texas and in D.C. He met a political figure while working in Kleberg's office who was to become one of his most important patrons in the future, Alvin Wirtz.

When Johnson ran for his first elected office as congressman, he turned to the former state senator, Alvin Wirtz, to ask for advice. Wirtz's counsel was to back FDR to the hilt (it was 1938), which he did, and got elected. Not only did Wirtz give him advice and guidance, he connected Lyndon over the years with a group of financial and social sponsors, the Brown brothers (construction) and Charles Marsh (newspapers) (Dugger, 1982).

He met and made himself so entertaining to FDR when he was elected to Congress that Roosevelt paved his way to major committees in Congress and was of great help in later years in his obtaining important measures for effecting economic and social relief for his Texas district—dams, electrification, and other projects. Johnson embraced FDR as his leader and for a while seemed to form a genuine identification, so that he espoused the social ideals of the New Deal and had friends of the same ilk—Abe Fortas, James Rowe, and Tommy Corcoran (Caro, 1983; Steinberg, 1973). Next as "political daddy" came Mister Sam Rayburn, the house leader. Johnson's attack on him was almost frontal; he invited Mister Sam to become a part of his and his bride Lady Bird's home. They became family for the single, isolated man. Lyndon became the son that Rayburn never had, and imbibed from him the political lore which Rayburn had in abundance.

However, as we have seen, Johnson's "loyalty" to any one of these mentors was not permanent; so that when FDR had a dispute with Jack Garner, whom Rayburn had to support, Johnson, under orders from FDR, turned on his patron Rayburn (Evans & Novak, 1966).

Johnson's next major alter ego was Richard Russell when Johnson got elected as senator. He had already been in contact through Wirtz with Texas real estate and oil barons and was on his way to becoming a radio mogul. Once elected to the senatorship, his liberal identifications were discarded in favor of the Southern and Texas senator image to assure the backings of the oil and gas interests he had previously fought as a New Deal congressman. Insinuating himself into Russell's good graces was not difficult for Johnson; he simply reperformed the Rayburn operation. Russell was also a bachelor and once again Johnson adopted him. This courtship took a little longer, since Russell was a more aloof figure than Mister Sam. Johnson had to tone down his manner and speech. He also had to make clear that he was a Southerner by advocating the filibuster, and an anti-Communist, although it was a relatively lengthy process (Caro, 1983; Kearns, 1976; Steinberg, 1973).

Russell succumbed to these maneuvers, and Johnson could begin to secure another transfusion of power. With Russell's backing, he became minority leader of the Senate, and then, with a little luck, became the Senate Majority leader, and achieved his greatest fame. Of course it ultimately became clear to Russell, as it had to Rayburn and the New Dealers, that Johnson was not "one of them." When he deserted the Southern bloc in 1957 to become the major mover behind the civil rights legislation, he was exposed again as an opportunist, not a devotee of the Southern cause (Evans & Novak, 1966).

It might be asked, isn't this all just standard politicking? Isn't the question that always arises of a politician, "Is he *sincere?*" But in the basic human qualities of gratitude, loyalty, affectionate regard, constancy in certain fundamental values, we find in Johnson a singular void. If he could veer about, as he did, without compunction, it was because there was not sufficient "self" to commit to another person or to a cause beyond that self.

When Johnson lost the race to become the Democratic candidate for president to Jack Kennedy in 1960, he accepted the vice-presidential slot and went on to help win the election for the party, himself, and Jack Kennedy. But the vice presidency turned out to be a bitter pill for Johnson to swallow since it was clear to everyone early in the Kennedy administration that his job was to be decorative. All reports indicate that with the loss of the power that sustained him so long as Majority Leader in the Senate, Johnson became deflated and looked and acted clinically depressed (Kearns, 1976).

With the resumption of his leadership as President, Johnson became the happy warrior once again, albeit with all the old eccentricities on display: the hyperactivity, the clamoring and invective-hurling, and the wheeling and dealing. Since he himself was now the parent figure for the Western world, it was difficult to set someone up to be his leader; but Johnson did have people to idealize, as well as people with whom he shared thoughts and exchanged ideas in a manner akin to transfusion. He was able to secure the services of Robert McNamara in the role he played with John F. Kennedy. McNamara was the consummate executive with the razor-sharp mind, always ready with an array of statistics, graphs, and projections, and with answers

to questions. Johnson, early in his presidency, was under McNamara's tutelage on Vietnam.

McGeorge Bundy, Maxwell Taylor, and Dean Rusk
all were extraordinary men, much admired by Johnson,
and all at one time or another idealized (Halberstam,
1972). LBJ of course had confidants not in his employ
during the presidency: Abe Fortas and Clark Clifford
were among the most important to him and the most
influential. Fortas, especially before and after he became a Supreme Court justice, was the man closest to a
brother that Johnson ever had. Finally, as the Vietnam
conflict continued to tear at the nation, Johnson totally
lost all support, and left the White House in a self state
of profoundly lowered worth.

CRITICAL ANALYSIS

Johnson, like Shakespeare's Richard III, seems
more a caricature of a man than a real-life person, who
revealed scant capacities for empathy and dialogue.
Even a casual observer could not fail to observe that this
man was always in motion and always engrossed in
activities that centered on himself: his appetites for applause, for direction, etc. We now seek to answer the
question, how did these unusual behaviors come to be
part of Johnson's mature life?

Lyndon Johnson's life was dominated, round the
clock, seven days a week, by his self seeking the contacts and activities that would keep him in equilibrium.
These behaviors, as we have described, reflected the
lacunae in his self that he attempted to fill during his
lifetime.

One major aspect of self-enfeeblement in Johnson

was in the area of self-regard. As was described, this part of the self is ordinarily developed early in life in the form of an infant's already expressing an "adequate" sense of worth by the time infancy is completed (24 months). Johnson's undiminished search for mirroring throughout his lifetime reflect an early fixation: an unconscious fueling of behaviors designed to obtain these narcissistic supplies of worth. The tragedy in these repetitious archaic strivings and the accompanying behaviors is that they never accomplish the task of filling the unfilled self.

Two major variables are associated with this Sisyphan outcome: The self is searching for and will never find the *actual* archaic selfobject; the second interference with the desired gratification is the element of defense transference. Johnson, like all fixated persons, in his search to obtain his archaic striving, was unconsciously attempting to find his original missing selfobject in all his transactions in which he was looking for mirroring, mother Rebekah. When he became aware that he was not to be gratified in this quest for his actual archaic selfobject, he would, as all fixated people do, decamp and look elsewhere, and again and again be disappointed. He was unconsciously attempting to restructure and thereby retrieve the ancient scene; the infant on the lap of the goddess of his infancy: and therefore repetitively was disappointed in each of his renewed missions to attain mirroring.

The second interference with the acquisition of the mirroring supplies from an archaic selfobject was the element of the self-defense originally erected by the self to maintain a barrier against the unrewarding or disappointing or feared selfobject. In its recreated form as a transference, the self now invests the transference selfobject with those fearful features of the original selfobject and then defends itself by limiting its openness against this potentially harmful selfobject. Johnson's repetitious wish for mirroring and his defense transference was manifested by his seeking recognition wherever he went but never allowing himself to be "owned" by anyone; he never allowed himself fully to unfold to *anyone*.

In the same way, Johnson demonstrated his unremitting attempts to acquire a guru and fill out his self, but again the same two variables interfered. He sought out political and social and financial father figures through his life but, again, these missions were bound to fail since he was seeking out the *actual* archaic *idealized* selfobject, a mixture of Grandpa Sam and Father Sam; and he was further stopped by the defense transference against allowing himself totally to unfold to any leader. He did attempt to secure many people's power and ideals but eventually he could only drain their power and leave.

In this fashion he received a partial transfusion from Evans, Kleberg, Wirtz, FDR, Rayburn, Russell, Alice Marsh, Charles Marsh, Herman Brown, Robert McNamara, and McGeorge Bundy. We also noted that Johnson needed to be reassured that his mother's mission and idealized functions would continue interminably, transferred from the image of her archaic self to her present self, and from the image of his archaic self to his present self, so that he could always reach out and she would be there.

Another major aspect of the fixation process in general and therefore in Lyndon Johnson was the difficulty in deriving sufficient gratifications from the here-and-now sources of self-supplies. The attraction to the past gratifications, added to the diminutive attraction to the gratifications in the present sum up to the process of psychological or developmental fixation. To Johnson, as to any person who has a psychological fixation, whenever a psychological need becomes apparent, the attraction to the past becomes activated.

When you are in need and you unwittingly turn, like Johnson, to the archaic sources of worth, your strategy is to get close to the archaic selfobject who you "know" will ultimately react to gratify you. Moreover, your tactics to obtain these gratifications are particularly structured as in the past to realize these strivings. Thus Johnson, in the midst of his wish to obtain the affirmation, approval, admiring or guidance-direction gratifications which he was hungry to secure, would show the special behaviors of the youngster: clamoring for attention, subservience, exaggerated interest, exaggerations to proclaim his worth, duplicity to conceal any evidence of inferiority, flattery to evoke direction from the potential selfobject, total control of his staff or aides so that no one left his side.

These behaviors represent turning away of the tactics and the strategies that Johnson would pursue if his wants to obtain interest were confined to here-and-now gratifications. Johnson's uneasiness at immersing himself without restraint in any human bond never allowed him to overcome the loneliness with which he lived. The clamoring, the overcontrol, the wheeling and dealing, the eternal vigilance—all these represent the turning away from so-called mature ways of obtaining direction, warmth, love, and camaraderie, which are based on the unfolding of one's longings and strivings to suitable objects and selfobjects.

The fixations that dominated Johnson's intrapsychic

life urge us to attempt an understanding of the process which clearly was out of his awareness. These ancient modes of pursuing life were certainly familiar and safe to Lyndon since childhood. He knew how to get to Rebekah by clamoring, even though it was never adequate to fill his needs; he knew how to get power by being subservient to his mentors since adolescence, even though he could never derive sufficient power in these bonds. He never had to get totally immersed in a love relationship, and lose control. These archaic modes of contact and involvement had been going on for so long that for Lyndon they were the tactics by which he adapted to his world. Turning to the familiar and the safe are of course partial explanations of the process of fixation of modes of experience and behavior. In order to be complete, the explanations have to include the study of the particular central nervous system under scrutiny, and its capacity to form neuronal circuits of human and nonhuman sources of gratification, the unknown functions of the brain that define the psychological fixity of any particular self.

SUMMARY REMARKS

It is the empathic diagnosis of this volume based on the accumulated data that Lyndon Johnson, a courageous and resourceful person and president in much of what he did, had no choices in the way he lived his life; he was dominated by unconscious restrictions and by unconscious attractions to pursue an existence of grabbing at recognition and at leadership in the only manner available to him. His inner needs for maintaining a milieu of approval so influenced his interactional world that any activity of his or anyone under his purview that would possibly invoke criticism—ultimately for him the withholding of approval—made him so fearful as to trigger a rage reaction.

The self-need for affirmation and its counterpart, the fear of censure, became hypertrophied as he became the major decision maker of the Western world. The nature of leadership as president of course entails an exposure from which Johnson recoiled but which, as leader of our republic, could not be dismissed. A more important facet of the credentials for leadership is that the citizens trust that the leader's decisions reflect his empathy for the needs of the people in the major decisions he makes, certainly those in which lives are at stake. Implicit in this assumption is that the self of the leader of the republic will be a highly developed self, a minimum of deficits, as one of the necessary credentials to secure and maintain the high office.

To Johnson, the petitioning for direct acceptance of him and his longings and strivings—the major pathway to fulfilling life—was not a pathway of intercourse that was open. He could not and did not engage in the relatedness with people based on a mutuality of empathy and its vicissitudes of dialogue and endearments. His interactional life was in the main without object relationships. That is, he was not involved with people as unique entities with distinct styles and interests to appreciate and share. His motive in understanding differences in people was based on his desire to create an intelligence file to use in inveigling them into some project or action he wished them to execute.

To Johnson, so often caught up in his own game plan, people were interchangeable, not discrete individuals with self-strivings that required empathy. Thus en-

counters with people too often became encounters with
selfobjects in which, as in all selfobject encounters, it is
their function for the self that is sought, not their individu-
ality. These selfobject functions—affirming, applauding, admiring—surely would be forthcoming if only he
were a *successful* performer, or demander, or seducer or
schemer!

Is this self of Lyndon Johnson, as we have defined
it, compatible with the requirements for leadership in
a democracy? If our leaders do not reflect carefully
enough—cannot empathize—with our shared needs in
this culture, at this juncture in history, then how can
they be said to fulfill the criteria for a president of a
democracy?

We have attempted in these chapters, spurred by
our research inquiries to gather sufficient data to make a
statement about Johnson's uniqueness that is comprehensive and valid:

> Johnson's formed self was a self that manifested many
> features of old longings and old ways to procure gratifications
> and was therefore doomed to repeat ancient disappointments;
> since the past could never be revived.

We turn now to Johnson's experiences and conduct
in the Vietnam war where the self limitations of the
thirty-sixth president were exposed to the misfortune of
the nation and its youth.

Chapter 6

JOHNSON AND
THE VIETNAM WAR

On August 2 and 4, 1964, North Vietnamese naval forces in the Gulf of Tonkin were reported to have attacked United States destroyers. On August 8, 1964, during a press conference at the LBJ ranch, President Johnson made the following comments:

> The situation created by unprovoked aggression against our naval forces on the high seas remains serious, but there have been no further incidents in the last 24 hours. We, of course, remain fully alert against any attempt to renew or widen the attacks from any source.
>
> It is important for us all to understand that these attacks at sea are only part of a basic pattern of aggression which had already shown itself against the people and government of South Vietnam and its people and the government of Laos. Our actions this week make clear not only our determination to give a clear and positive reply to aggression at sea, but our general determination to resist and repel aggression in the area as a whole. That is the meaning also of the resolution adopted yesterday by the Congress with almost complete unanimity.
>
> Finally, let me repeat again and again that in all our actions, our purpose is peace. (Presidential Press Conference, p. 188)

The Tonkin Gulf incident had its inception in January when Johnson gave permission to plan a series of covert activities against North Vietnam under the code name of "34A." McGeorge Bundy was ordered to oversee the operations. One such operation was to send South Vietnamese PT boats to raid North Vietnamese naval installations along the coast. On July 31, South Vietnamese PT boats had raided two North Vietnamese bases. At the same time, the American destroyer *Maddox* was on its way to the same location, the North Vietnam coast. Its mission was to provoke the North Vietnam radar system by electronically simulating an attack. When they turned on *their* radar in response, our side could then locate their radar installations.

Two days later, when the *Maddox* was some 13 miles from a North Vietnam island in the Gulf of Tonkin, three North Vietnamese PT boats attacked, and a fight ensued (Evans & Novak, 1968; Goulden, 1969; Halberstam, 1983). The following day the *Maddox* and another vessel, the *C. Turner Joy*, were ordered back into the same area; immediately, so the story goes, they were fired on. These incidents became known as the Tonkin Gulf incidents. They are central to the onset of the Vietnam war since, directly after these incidents were reported, the initial United States bombing of North Vietnam began, opening the way to the undeclared war in Vietnam that would bring so much death and destruction.

Here is the key point we wish to advance: The manner in which these events were reported and dealt with demonstrated the workings of the Johnson use of military power and the use of human lives to protect himself against censure.

What were Johnson's priorities as he entered this stage of his presidency? Prior to the Tonkin Gulf incident in the summer of 1964, Johnson was involved in many matters relating to the domestic projects of the Great Society program, and organizing his campaign to run against Barry Goldwater. Various observers of the Tonkin Gulf events concluded that these hostilities, regardless of who fired on whom, or who was the essential instigator, were then used by Johnson for political or psychological gain. Halberstam concluded that the incident in the Gulf of Tonkin "provided the factor of patriotism that he had sought" to overcome any congressional backlash, either by the liberals for maintaining troops in Vietnam, or by the conservatives for not quelling Communism in Southeast Asia (p. 456). Evans and Novak called his actions of retaliatory air strikes a "shrewd political act shoring up Johnson against the Republican campaign charge that he was soft on Communism" (p. 553). Goulden's conclusion was that the entire Tonkin Gulf incident and its dubious attacks on the United States' vessels were pretexts manufactured to adopt a resolution to support escalation of the war which Johnson could use after his election (Goulden, 1969).

What Johnson did after the second day of "unprovoked attacks" on the *Maddox* and the *C. Turner Joy* was to order retaliatory air strikes against North Vietnamese PT installations. He also used these incidents to call together congressional leaders on August 4—including his opponent, Barry Goldwater—and enlist their support. He, of course, did not mention the spy ship activities of the *Maddox* (Goulden, 1969; Halberstam, 1972); but did tell them of his retaliation plans. He talked of a "limited" retaliation. Next, he laid plans to secure a congressional resolution that same night. Put together by McGeorge Bundy, it was rushed to Congress and in just two days received the combined Senate-

House vote of 502 to 2 (Wayne Morse of Oregon and Ernest Gruening of Alaska voted against).

Johnson's major agent in the management of the resolution was an old crony, Senator William Fulbright, the chairman of the Senate Foreign Relations Committee. During his days as the Majority leader, Johnson referred to Fulbright as my "Secretary of State" (Halberstam, 1972, p. 505).

Fulbright's management of the resolution through the Joint Foreign Relations Committee, the Armed Services Committee, and then the full Senate, proved to be a key factor battling against the forces of such mighty foes as Senators Wayne Morse, Ernest Gruening, Gaylord Watson, and Sherman Cooper. The Johnson team had exhibited perfidiousness to the congressional Committees of Congress through McNamara's disingenuous testimony which claimed, among other assertions, that the *Maddox* was outside the 12-mile limit; the full story of the United States provoking the North Vietnamese forces had been left out.

Fulbright himself was lied to and misled. Morse, receiving a last-minute tip from a source at the Pentagon, had begged Fulbright to delay the passage of the resolution and allow for further hearings. Morse had, apparently, been told the *Maddox* was a spy ship, closer to the coastline than McNamara had indicated and, thereby, illegally positioned (Goulden, 1969; Halberstam, 1972). But the patriotism issue was foremost in everyone's mind on August 4 to August 7, and the resolution passed.

The Tonkin Bay Resolution gave Johnson legal authority to pursue war. This spelled a victory for Johnson and his now-compromised team, who knew what they had perpetrated on the Congress and the people. However, it also marked the beginning of a hostile and bitterly contested opposition to Johnson and his administration. Ironically, the leader was Fulbright, who felt personally betrayed by the Johnson treachery. The opposition to the war began in large part in the Senate Foreign Relations Committee, in reaction to their discovery of the Tonkin Bay schemes, since it was now known that the president and his aides could not be trusted.

These reactions did not surface at once; directly after the Tonkin Bay episode and the Tonkin Bay Resolution, Johnson's popularity soared, since he was the man who would not react to ordinary Communist provocation, and would not send Americans to do what "Asian boys" should do (Evans & Novak, 1968, p. 532). Goldwater was perceived as the dangerous person who would not hesitate to take us immediately into a land war, even to the extent of utilizing nuclear weapons. Thus, Johnson became the recognized peace candidate. Johnson was quoted as saying during the 1964 presidential campaign:

> We don't want our boys to do the fighting for Asian boys. We are not about to send American boys nine or ten thousand miles away from home to do what Asian boys ought to be doing to protect themselves. (Evans & Novak, 1968, p. 532)

Immediately after the election, Johnson did nothing further to heat up the military operations in Vietnam; the next phase of the escalation came after the Vietcong raid on the American air base at Pleiku on February 7, 1965.

Before we take up the next phase of "Lyndon's War," as it began to be called, it is important to recognize the psychological implications of what we have already observed: the entry into the bombing and, more important, the manner in which Johnson and his new team of McGeorge Bundy (special aide to Johnson), Robert McNamara (Secretary of Defense), and Dean Rusk (Secretary of State) pursued their aims in pushing the United States into the beginning of the Vietnamese war.

Johnson's motivations to begin the retaliatory bombing in August of 1964 were complex, a juggling act of ensuring that censure of him would not be unduly harsh. On the one hand, the reactionaries in Congress, the Republicans as well as the conservative Democrats, would not admonish him for being soft on Communism. The liberals in Congress and elsewhere would be convinced that Johnson was operating with restraint in a patriotic manner, and American boys would not be shot at, by anyone.

The psychological issue at stake in these decisions was the chronically heightened sensitivity of Johnson to censure from the left, right, and everywhere. He had continued the covert operations of his predecessors, which included the spy ship operations of the *Maddox*, thereby keeping up the pressure against the omnipresent Communist threat to take over all of Vietnam. The North Vietnamese attacked the *Maddox* because they believed that the *Maddox* was part of the South Vietnamese actions against their coastal bases; at least so it was stated by navy commanders in the area (Goulden, 1969). The *Maddox*, of course, *was* a hostile ship; her mission *was* to spy. Johnson's reaction to this event was that he *had* to demonstrate a firm resolve against Communist attackers immediately to avoid censure.

Of course, to be soft on Communism was a particularly unusual charge against Johnson, given his usual—and public—stands in Congress and elsewhere against people with leftist leanings already in the government and those, like Leland Olds, who wished to be part of the government and who Johnson attacked unmercifully (Caro, 1983). Another of Johnson's concerns centered on his oft-stated fear of losing a country to Communism while he had the watch, akin to Truman's "loss" of China (Kearns, 1976).

The self reactions of fear of loss of the approval from the group self of the nation evoked the decisions he made at the outset of the Vietnam tragedy, the "Tonkin Bay phenomenon." What was missing in his decision making here and later was the empathy and concern for the lives that would be affected by becoming involved in hostilities, rather than his need to be seen as "patriotic." It was, of course, the unfolding of Johnson's unique reactions to the group self of the nation in which he unconsciously began to experience himself and his actions as if he were on trial proceedings to determine his worth—either to be approved or censured by the nation acting as his judge.

Thus, the crucial decision to enter into the "quagmire" at this stage, as Halberstam was to call the Vietnam involvement (Halberstam, 1965), was made, in our view, to provide Johnson with the mantle of a patriot rushing to protect American lives and interests. In this way he could neutralize Barry Goldwater's claim as the Super-American. Empathic observations of the strategies and tactics involved in these "political" decisions urge us again to consider what was at stake from the point of view of Johnson's self-interests. To begin with, the decision was, first and last, one that was fueled by the self-concern of the leader. This, as we have now witnessed throughout the history of Lyndon Johnson, was central in his dealings throughout his life. This constituted the major strategy of his involvement in Vietnam; the preservation of his self cohesion against any potential destroyers of his self. Other actions he took to maintain his self-equilibrium were directed to ensure that the public display of his self, in this case the military actions, were free from any possibility of censure, and sufficiently exemplary to ensure the mirroring for which he lived. His motto became "whatever it takes," indicating that he would take whatever action was required to obtain applause and admiration.

Thus, ordering McNamara to stand before the Senate Foreign Relations Committee and lie—to lie before Congress—that the attacks on the *Maddox* were unprovoked, as he did in the press releases to the nation and in the quoted press conference on August 8, was necessary and clearly acceptable to Johnson. The orchestration of the theme of obtaining consensual validation for the air strikes by calling the congressional leaders was another tactic to afford him self-approval, not simply general sharing of a critical decision affecting many. Another tactic-for-mirroring and the corollary avoidance of censure, as noted previously, was to involve Senator Fulbright, who up to then had counted Johnson a friend, in his scheme to obtain a quick passage of the Gulf of Tonkin Resolution, which gave Johnson extraordinary powers to wage war without a declaration of war by Congress.

Fulbright was later railed at on the floor of Congress by antagonists of the Tonkin Resolution—Senators Morse and Nelson—and had to accept their criticism that he had been wrong to go along with Lyndon Johnson (Halberstam, 1972). And so, to his senatorial friends and colleagues, to reporters, to the people of the United States, to the world, Johnson lied and lied and entered into these acts of hostility to protect himself against possible criticism and to obtain an infusion of self-regard.

Moreover, and much the more important issue involved in these "political" actions—which were, as we have seen, "self-concerned" actions—the self absorbed in its own needs, as was Johnson's, operated without any empathic lens. Empathic considerations for the lives he endangered or lost did not influence the actions of Lyndon Johnson in the decision to order air strikes or in many other so-called political actions. To be empathic with the needs of those he commanded or with those on whom he would inflict violence, would have resulted in a different set of decisions.

Preoccupied as Johnson was with protecting himself against censure, he made decisions to maintain secrecy that were to be ultimately to his disadvantage. Fulbright, for example, became his sworn enemy after the Gulf of Tonkin Resolution. Taking Fulbright into his confidence might have made him an ally, rather than the enemy he became to Johnson and the war. Fulbright and his Foreign Relations Committee became the seat of the liberal antagonism to the Vietnam War. Decisions of the nature Johnson or any other leader made in the Tonkin Bay actions, without the empathic addition to one's decision making, it seems to us, are always destructive and dangerous to the group under such leadership. Barbara Tuchman, the historian, might have been speaking of this dangerous absence of empathy in Johnson's self when she wrote:

> Forceful and domineering, a man infatuated with himself, Johnson was afflicted in his conduct of Vietnam policy by three elements in his character: an ego that was insatiable and never secure, a bottomless capacity to use and impose the

powers of office without inhibition; a profound aversion, once
fixed on a course of action, to any contra-indications. (p. 311)

When Heinz Kohut discussed empathy as a tool for
observation, underscoring its necessity in the understanding of one's fellowman, he described those who
could not use empathy, in whom it had never been developed or adequately developed. He was referring to
those persons whose relationship with their caretakers
was grossly inadequate, so that due to their appetites
for continual input from their surround, which continued throughout their lives, they simply do not and never
did observe the others' needs. Kohut called these syn-
dromes *primary empathy deficits* (Kohut, 1971). Lyndon
Johnson exhibited these features in part in his dealings
with others' needs throughout his life; as he came to
take on more responsibility for the lives of more people,
his empathic deficits were shown more starkly.

To continue with the manner in which his personal
self traits were displayed in the Vietnam war, the shooting war was said to have begun on February 7, 1965,
when the Vietcong attacked the United States barracks
at Pleiku, and nine American soldiers were killed. The
bombing of the North started in full force in reaction to
this event, although Johnson's closest advisors had been
urging this for some time. In fact, McGeorge Bundy had
gone to Vietnam prior to the Pleiku attack and was there
to document personally to Johnson that retaliation was
now clearly in order (Halberstam, 1972).

The bare facts of the history of the war are well
known. After the decision for sustained bombing was
made and initiated on February 13, 1965, the military
requested troops to protect the Da Nang Air Base. A few
weeks later, Westmoreland requested additional troops.

In April 1965, there were 50,000 United States soldiers in South Vietnam (Kahin, 1987; Kearns, 1976).

In July 1965, the Johnson advisors presented Johnson with a set of recommendations necessary to pursue adequately the conflict in Vietnam, stressing that the expansion of troops to a force of 200,000 men was necessary to withstand the enemy forces, and prevent a takeover of South Vietnam. When Johnson acceded to these requests, the United States entered into what ultimately became the longest war in its history without a declaration of war, or any specific affirmation from the Congress (Kahin, 1987; Kearns, 1976).

The motives of McGeorge Bundy and Robert McNamara to the side, the military ambitions of Lyndon Johnson now became clear. Johnson himself wished to pursue a war plan in Vietnam and become the patriot who would drive out the "Communist devil" in Vietnam. To offer an overview of his aspirations and his fears over entering into the war:

1. Johnson, some observers noted, seemed to have been attracted since 1961 to the idea that a great stand against Communism had to be made by American forces in Asia, and that this could be his greatest contribution to mankind (Kahin, 1987). His views were expressed in a memo to President Kennedy reporting his findings and views of the situation in Southeast Asia at that time (1961). In that memo he stressed that firm action should be taken against the Communist forces (Evans & Novak, 1976). In his wish to be the hero of the great stand against Communism, Johnson was said to have been an enemy of early efforts at armistice in Vietnam proposed by China and the Soviet Union (Kahin, 1987). From this view, Johnson's reprisal bombing, the

"Flaming Dart" program, was not simply initiated by the events at Pleiku, but by his own ambitions as well.

2. The more accepted story of the military history of the war has always emphasized that Johnson's advisors played the key role in the escalation of the war, especially the two "hawks," McGeorge Bundy and Robert McNamara. In fact, the conventional history has always stressed that Johnson was reluctant to commit the military to a land war in Southeast Asia, especially in 1965, as he was getting ready to launch the programs of the Great Society (Halberstam, 1972).

3. What were his fears of entering into a war in Vietnam? A potent restrainer on his full-fledged entry into the war was his concern that China would come to the aid of North Vietnam, since Johnson suspected they had treaty arrangements.

The major restrainer, however, was his ever-present fear of losing his Great Society programs for economic development:

> "I was determined to keep the war from shattering that dream," Johnson later said, "which meant I simply had no choice but to keep my foreign policy in the wings. I knew Congress as well as I know Lady Bird, and I knew that the day it exploded into a major debate on the war, that day would be the beginning of the end of the Great Society...I was determined to be a leader of war and a leader of peace. I refused to let my critics push me into choosing one or the other. I wanted both, I believed in both, and I believed America had the resources to provide for both. After all, our country was built by pioneers who had a rifle in one hand to kill their enemies and an ax in the other to build their homes and provide for their families." (Kearns, 1976, pp. 282, 283)

He revealed a mixture of concerns and ambitions about his decisions in these thoughts he spoke to Doris Kearns:

For this time there would be Robert Kennedy out in front leading the fight against me, telling everyone that I had betrayed John Kennedy's commitment to South Vietnam. That I had let a democracy fall into the hands of the Communists. That I was a coward. An unmanly man. A man without a spine. Oh, I could see it coming all right. Every night when I fell asleep I would see myself tied to the ground in the middle of a long, open space. In the distance, I could hear the voices of thousands of people. They were all shouting at me and running toward me: "Coward! Traitor! Weakling!" They keep coming closer. They began throwing stones. At exactly that moment, I would generally wake up...terribly shaken. But there was more. You see, I was as sure as any man could be that once we showed how weak we were, Moscow and Peking would move in a flash to exploit our weakness. They might move independently or they might move together. But move, they would—whether through nuclear blackmail, through subversion, with regular armed forces or in some other manner. As nearly as anyone can be certain of anything, I knew they couldn't resist the opportunity to expand their control over the vacuum of power we would leave behind us. And so would begin World War III. So you see, I was bound to be crucified either way I moved.

And so, as always in Johnson's preoccupations, there was the ever-present fear of exposing even a scintilla of ineptitude. He was, however, heartened by his associates. Tom Wicker reported:

> He would look around him and see in Bob McNamara that it was technologically feasible, in McGeorge Bundy that it was intellectually respectable, and in Dean Rusk that it was historically necessary. (p. 183)

4. Johnson's resolution of his fears and his ambitions to enter into the Vietnam conflict and triumph were resolved in a characteristic way. Once again he took measures to protect himself against any criticism of his action and its sequelae, public humiliation and dismissal from office, in the following steps:

In opposition to his inner circle of advisers, he decided against disclosing to the country the actual military situation in Vietnam and what his war policies would entail. Although he and his advisers were planning to initiate a full-scale war, he did not put the economy on a wartime footing by asking Congress for higher taxes, nor did he order the mobilization of reservists. Most significantly, he did not go to the nation with the announcement that we were entering into a major war, and certainly one that would strain our economic and human resources.

The secrecy that Lyndon displayed as well as his other tactics to avoid disclosure—the duplicity, the omissions, the gibes and sarcasm to dissuade questioners—were all part of his armamentarium for fending off the hostiles who would uncover the current project, or action, or truth that he was guarding. These fears of disclosure that influenced Johnson's thinking during his tenure as president—they were not as prominent in his senatorial days—reflected his omnipresent fear of being *weak*. The fear of disclosure evoked the fear of loss of control which called up the need to be in control at all times.

To Johnson, there was the ever-present possibility that he would be "caught" harboring an attitude, or making a decision, or engaged in an activity that someone in power would criticize. Thus, for example, he would insist he drank bourbon when everyone knew he drank scotch—a Southerner or Texan drinks bourbon. He insisted that Richard Goodwin, his speech writer and a former speech writer in the Kennedy administration, wrote only two speeches for him. Might someone look askance at his need to have Kennedy's writers; couldn't he get his own? He would change speeches immediately if he heard that someone had learned the contents of the speech; some hostile person might attack and print it before he had given the speech. In all these behaviors, Lyndon Johnson revealed the increasing fears that invaded his self, especially after he assumed the presidency and became a solo act, exposed at all turns, still trying to hide his self from exposures for fear of punishment from a hostile surround (Evans & Novak, 1969; Halberstam, 1972; Kearns, 1976; Sidey, 1968).

The prevailing wisdom about Johnson's stylistic difficulties as he moved into the job of the chief executive was that he was so used to the deal-making in the Senate that he could not easily adjust to the need to inform the people so as to obtain consensus with his new clients, the people of the United States. Secrecy, duplicity, exaggerations—all these tactics, perhaps necessary in waging war in the Senate, were unnecessary and contraindicated in the formation of a trusting relationship between the President of the United States and his fellow citizens. Other rationalizations for Johnson's secrecy and duplicitous behavior on the Vietnam war was that, in his view, as already noted, the financing of the Great Society would be endangered.

In countering these "rational" arguments and others of the same ilk, we are advancing the thesis that Johnson's behaviors as president were determined by increasing fears of disclosure—*not* of losing the Great Society nor of disclosure of any specific program, but of disclosure of his *own* self-of-inadequacy.

In fact, either due to greater awareness of him through media coverage, or as an intensification in Johnson's self-doubts, his self-sensitivity to rebuke and to disappointment was intensified when he moved to the White House in 1964. His needs for selfobject support increased, accompanied as always by his fears of the unfolding of these self states of need for mirroring. In effect, Johnson showed an intensification of his chronic narcissistic (self-worth) deficits throughout his presidency—always needy and never safe in being in need, since the need was for him always associated with repudiation.

Nowhere were these dynamics played out more clearly than in the Tet offensive started by the Vietcong in 1968.

JOHNSON AND THE TET OFFENSIVE

On January 31, 1968, in an offensive outburst that permanently altered the future of the United States' effort in Vietnam, the enemy (the Vietcong and the North Vietnamese armies) launched a series of attacks throughout South Vietnam. The surprise element, apart from the failure of intelligence from our usual military sources, was due to the official reports coming from Vietnam to the United States at that time that the military balance had begun to swing to our side. The enemy was said to have been "weakened" by our search-and-destroy policy, aimed at attrition of the North Vietnamese war machine. In fact, Johnson's initial reaction (February 2, 1968) to the Tet offensive was that it had been "a complete failure" militarily and psychologically (Harper, 1985, p. 140).

His words were premature; they were also inaccurate. The Tet offensive was a "success" in that many civilian and military lives were lost and much property destroyed due to the efforts of the "weakened enemy." It was an even greater success in evoking the counterkilling of civilians and counterdestruction of homes that was unleashed by our troops and our firepower. Whole cities were decimated—for example, the ancient religious and cultural center of Hue—in an effort to destroy the enemy. Massive civilian casualties resulted from the attempt to destroy the enemy.

Moreover, the spectacle of the unleashed power of the "beaten" enemy which was shown on the nightly TV evoked a wave of outrage in the American public which had been told that the U.S. forces were winning the war. The public outcry was now matched by the growing dissension in the Johnson team, culminating in Johnson's March 31, 1968 speech announcing his withdrawal from any consideration of standing for the Democratic nomination for the presidency.

As ever, Johnson's self-concerns influenced the decision making throughout the Tet offensive, and in no small way led to the repeated failures of Johnson and his administration to arrange for a peace agreement. Thus, Johnson's initial reaction to the Tet offensive in his public announcements was to firm up his resolve that the basic policy was not to be questioned: we would be victorious in Vietnam.

It should be reemphasized here that the initial raison d'être for entering the war was to interfere with the sweep of Communism in Southeast Asia and secure the integrity of the people of South Vietnam; our official purpose in entering Vietnam was not to win a military victory. However, Johnson's covert agenda for military victory was revealed as he colluded with Westmoreland's ground strategy to search and destroy enemy units and ultimately win the war. Johnson's failure to respond to a growing consortium within the country (TV, radio, newspapers, students, campus uprisings, challenges by statesmen and influential scholars), and advisers who were not in agreement with him and urgently pleaded for the war to end, became more pronounced as the Tet offensive continued.

The strategy (Hoopes, 1973) of the NVN and Vietcong armies in the Tet offensive was three-pronged: One drive was to attack Saigon and other cities; another to attack the U.S. base at Khesanh; and the third to invade and capture the countryside left occupied by the South Vietnam government troops hurrying into the cities to defend them against the North Vietnamese. Hoopes and other military students of the war believed then and later that our ground strategy was flawed, and desperately in need of reevaluation by the Joint Chiefs of Staff, the Secretary of State (McNamara), the other military advisers and, of course, Johnson. Hoopes and others believed that Westmoreland's search-and-destroy policy in the uninhabited portions of Vietnam (e.g., the Annamite mountain chain) should be abolished. The emphasis in the view of increasing numbers of observers was to "concentrate on the population centers and curtail American casualties" (Hoopes, 1973, p. 146). In February 1968, Johnson would not listen to any petitions for reexamination of the established military policy, nor would he listen to any query about his commander.

An instructive and tragic example of Johnson's resolution to hang onto a failing strategy was played out at the Khesanh military base, where the enemy was on the attack in great force. The official strategy was to stand and attempt to win the day; an alternative strategy would have been to withdraw and utilize the 7,000 combat troops for combat in the South Vietnamese countryside now being overtaken by the V.C. troops. However, no one (not the Joint Chiefs nor any opposing advisers) could make an impact on Johnson's devotion to Westmoreland and his strategy of winning the war. Actually, it was not until April 1, 1968, that the enemy forces withdrew from Khesanh. They had been pounded by the heaviest bombing than had been dropped on any other target in the *entire* history of warfare. As Hoopes said, "...by no means did it redeem the Westmoreland strategy. What it did was to retrieve a serious blunder by the...application of airpower" (p. 214).

Now, at the end of February, 1968, the country was reeling with the daily barrage of the news of the heavy losses of young men on both sides. The credibility gap had widened immeasurably in response to the news of the offensive able to be mounted by the "weakened enemy" (Halberstam, 1972). Johnson's speeches became more hortatory during that time: "...Persevere in Vietnam we will and we must. The enemy has failed because we have answered aggression's onslaught with one strong voice, 'No retreat' they have said" (Hoopes, 1973, p. 157).

The first month of the Tet offensive ended in an impasse. The North Vietnamese armies and the Vietcong had slowed down with the enormous casualties that they suffered (between 28,000 to 40,000 KIA); *but* they had occupied 35 cities at different times and 25,000 civilians were killed; enormous physical destruction had taken place. The loss to the Administration's credibility was a death blow, perhaps best captured by Frank McGee, the NBC anchorman, who asserted that the war was being lost in relation to the stated goal of the war to hold off the Communists in order for a non-Communist South Vietnam to flourish. Now, with thousands homeless and the government weak, the prospects for freedom in South Vietnam were more distant (Hoopes, 1973).

When General Westmoreland stated at the end of the first month of the Tet offensive that he needed 206,000 men to complete his mission, he started a wave of protest in the United States that ended when Johnson finally agreed to hold peace talks with the enemy. Sent by Johnson to receive an on-site report from Westmoreland, General Wheeler reported that fighting by the enemy was unimpeded and continuing. The *reactions* to these "force requirements" — quickly advertised nationwide — now unneutralized and unrationalized by the absence of persuasive arguments of the departing Robert McNamara, included a surprisingly strong showing by Senator Eugene McCarthy in a presidential primary in New Hampshire. Perhaps the request for more troops, indicating our failure in Vietnam, influenced Robert Kennedy to run for the presidency (Hoopes, 1973).

When Clark Clifford came on board, after Robert McNamara left, Johnson thought he had taken on a stalwart friend of himself and the Vietnam war. Clifford, however, soon became the most effective enemy of the war and in no small way contributed to Johnson's resignation speech (declaring he would not be a candidate for the presidency) only one month after he became Secretary of Defense. When Clifford presented a special task force's recommendations to Johnson that had considered Westmoreland's request for over 200,000 men, he stated that he and the task force had now developed doubts about the ground strategy of Westmoreland and the effectiveness of the bombing campaign as it was executed.

As expected, the long-standing warm relationship between LBJ and Clifford rapidly cooled and soon deteriorated. Johnson actually stopped seeing him for personal sessions in the summer of 1968, when Clifford continued to press him to call a total halt to the bombing (Hoopes, 1973).

Johnson's critics and their diatribes continued to become more evident in the following months. Bobby Kennedy announced his desire to campaign for the presidency in March of 1968. Arthur Goldberg, our ambassador to the U.N., sent a private "bombing halt" memorandum to Johnson which Johnson rejected. Johnson also learned in March that the Westmoreland request would raise the defense budget by $2.5 billion in 1968 and by $10 billion in 1969 (Hoopes, 1973), and thereby endanger his Great Society program.

At this point in the war, Townsend Hoopes, the Assistant Secretary of the Air Force, sent a memorandum to the new Secretary of Defense, Clark Clifford. It contained a comprehensive overview of the difficulties that would be engendered in continuing the existing war policies, and concluded:

> Anything resembling a clean-cut military victory in Vietnam appears possible only at the price of literally destroying South Vietnam, tearing apart the social and political fabric of our country, alienating our European friends and gravely weakening the whole free world structure of relations and alliances.
>
> Judged against any rational scale of values, a military victory in Vietnam is, therefore, unfeasible at any price consistent with U.S. interests. (p. 195)

Yet another hostile confrontation came about for Johnson and his Vietnam policies in the form of the Fulbright Hearings. The Senate Foreign Relations Committee chaired by Senator Fulbright on March 12, 1968, opened the annual hearings on the Foreign Aid Bill.

After Dean Rusk and Robert McNamara gave their testi-
monies, they were confronted with the dissatisfaction of
the entire committee on the Vietnam war policies. Subsequently, both Clark Clifford and Paul Nitze, his
deputy, declined to testify. Both gave similar reasons,
either of having doubts or dissatisfactions with the war
policies.

As the pressure against him mounted, Johnson
reached out to another Cold War ally, Dean Acheson, for
support. Once again he was unsupported; Acheson, after consulting with the appropriate people at the CIA,
State, and the Joint Chiefs of Staff, came out against
the war. He told Johnson: (1) Westmoreland's policies
couldn't be realized before five years and would require
unlimited financial and personnel resources; (2) the
Joint Chiefs of Staff were not adequately informed (of
the field situation) to give him (Johnson) proper advice;
and (3) the country was against any furthering of the
war (Hoopes, 1973, p. 205).

What was Johnson's reaction to Clifford's and
Acheson's confrontations, Goldberg's bombing halt
memorandum, Bobby Kennedy's announcement of entry into the presidential race, and Gene McCarthy's
excellent showing in New Hampshire? As could be pre-
dicted on March 17 and March 20, 1968, he turned his
back on his detractors to give a hellfire-and-brimstone
speech against a defeatist attitude in Vietnam. On these
two occasions he said:

> Make no mistake about it, I don't want a man here to go
> back thinking otherwise—we are going to win. Those of you
> who think that you can save lives by moving the battlefield in
> from the mountains to the cities have another thought coming.
> (Hoopes, 1973, p. 206)

Clifford was now able to arrange a meeting of the

so-called Senior Advisers on Vietnam. He called in McGeorge Bundy, Abe Fortas, Dean Acheson, Arthur Goldberg, Maxwell Taylor, Cyrus Vance, and others who had been involved in policy-making on Vietnam. On March 26, their report was given to the President. McGeorge Bundy in a summary statement told Johnson that the group had achieved consensus on the resolution that the Vietnam policy should undergo significant change; it could not achieve its objectives without drawing on unlimited resources, which the country would not support. Johnson was apparently dismayed at the stature of those men who were in agreement with the overall consensus—men such as McGeorge Bundy, the Vietnam hawk, and Cyrus Vance, McNamara's right-hand man for years in the Pentagon (Hoopes, 1973).

Now Johnson was finally able to receive and agree to reading a "peace" address written by his speech writer Harry McPherson. In it he called for peace talks on the basis of bombing halts and deescalation of the entire armed-forces effort in Vietnam (McPherson, 1973).

Also in this speech of March 31, 1968, he surprised everyone in the audience with the announcement that he would not seek nor accept the nomination for President of the United States (Kearns, 1976).

It was not until October, however, that Clark Clifford and Cyrus Vance, acting in concert, were finally able to bring off a total bombing halt. Clark Clifford had to convince Johnson that it was important for his successor to have substantive grounds for negotiations, rather than possess the best military position at the time of the armistice (Hoopes, 1973).

It would seem that Johnson, to the moment he left office, could not acknowledge that the war policy had failed, nor that significant people had become disloyal. Until the last minute of the war that he ran, he kept up the military activity. Thus, up to the end, there were 550,000 troops active in Vietnam; there were 200 to 400 killed-in-action casualties per week; and the war budget was $30 billion per year up to the moment Johnson left office.

Once again we are face-to-face with the self traits of Johnson, his fear of failure and his fear of revealing ineptitude. Here was a tragic example of his flawed self in action. He could not cease and desist from his flawed military policy, which would constitute an admission of inadequacy, to Johnson an unacceptable circumstance.

DISCUSSION

The evidence amassed in this chapter points to decisions of entering and continuing a war made to maintain the self cohesion of Johnson. What we have adduced from the evidence surrounding the entry into the war was that LBJ was eager to enter the fray and pursue a land war with North Vietnam. A variety of motives suggest themselves that fueled this wish: His stated wish not to "lose" a country to the Communists, as did Truman in China; his wish to be true to the John F. Kennedy direction and avoid any charge that he deserted the Kennedy line; his wish to be the hero of Southeast Asia and thus a very desirable presidential candidate in 1968; his wish not to allow Barry Goldwater to outdo him as a superpatriot.

From the outset of the entry into the war, Johnson's particular self needs and self structures were in evidence. Yes, he did eagerly enter into the conflict, and the manner in which he did so revealed the Johnson self in action. Thus, he could and did agree, with very little validated data from the military, that our ships were attached. He could and did agree, we assume, with the untruths in the McNamara testimony that our ships were in international waters (outside the 12-mile limit) and that they were attacked in a totally unprovoked manner. All these assertions were known to be either false or without substantiation.

Beyond this, the capacity to enter into a serious conflict for political or self-aggrandizing motives, a conflict where lives were at stake, bespeaks of a self dangerously deficient in the minimal requirements for empathically driven leadership. As Johnson pursued his tactics to gain sufficient control of the nation and its resources to go to war, he used an old friend, Fulbright, as his straw boss. Without briefing him on what was involved, Johnson sent him out to stifle the opposition in Congress, utilizing the flag-waving approach of an imminent need for defense of "our boys" in Vietnam and the integrity of the SVN to push through the Tonkin Bay resolution so he could make war with impunity. No one in Congress expected Johnson at this point on August 7, 1964, to use the resolution to enter into a land war with the North Vietnamese; and certainly no one knew that Johnson wanted to win a military victory.

As the war was pursued in earnest through 1965, 1966, and 1967, the criticism of the war and the manner in which the war was being waged mounted through the North American continent on college campuses and in the streets of the United States. Criticism began to focus on the bombings and on the search-and-destroy ground missions of Westmoreland with its enormous loss of lives—American and Vietnamese. As the criticism of "Johnson's war" mounted in the media, on the campuses, and in Congress—especially in his former friend Fulbright's committee, the Senate Foreign Relations Committee, almost a country within a country—he began to show more and more reactions of depression and rage. In 1967, Johnson's difficulties at home increased as the battlefield wars were matched by the domestic difficulties in the country such as widespread inflation and the onset of race riots in the big cities in California and elsewhere.

Throughout those turbulent times, Johnson continued the style of leadership that featured *secrecy*, a way of operating that ultimately destroyed his administration's credibility throughout the country. He insisted on maintaining the illusion to his audience of Americans that we were not pursing a full-scale war in Southeast Asia. It followed, therefore, in his scheme of logic, that he need not inform the electorate of the conduct of this "limited" war. We now know that openly discussing the financial outlay of the war would, in Johnson's view, have damaged or challenged his Great Society plans.

Here were Johnson's revealed self-deficits at their most abysmal. A series of tragic blunders: a secret war financed in a semihidden manner through the Defense Department budget plans; a vast array of social programs (the Great Society) also requiring a vast outpouring of funds. Our President, uneasy about the social programs being threatened, but unwilling to propose tax increases to fund his programs, thus ushered in yet another domestic difficulty, inflation.

Leading the nation by secrecy and deception was not effective any more than it was to transform the executive branch into an armory where facts and policies were concealed. As can be gleaned from everything that

Johnson said in retrospect about his dealings with the
Vietnam war, he simply had no choice but to handle the
war in his characterological manner: maintaining control of everything—bombs, bullets, losses, the economic
drain—in his own hands. All the arguments he sum-
moned to rationalize his posture of perfidy were to no
avail as one becomes aware that the same tactics of secrecy and dissembling were present in the man from
childhood and, by the time of the ascension to the presidency, had, of course, long become self-syntonic (a familiar and acceptable action or trait).

Between 1967 and 1968, the tide for Johnson began
to turn significantly against him, the result of the social
and economic crisis now widespread in the country. The
onerous news of the war came ever closer through TV
and the press. Another disaster began in California: the
riots in the poverty-stricken communities. The first riot
began in August 1965, the precursor of over 100 such
riots over three "long hot summers" in which discon-
tented and poor elements of society led violent demon-
strations in the cities of the United States.

As events continued to demonstrate he had failed in
maintaining both his Great Society program and the
war in Vietnam, Johnson became more and more agitated and more and more accusative of people and the
institutions who "turned" against him. In describing
his reactions during this time, he told Doris Kearns:

> Two or three intellectuals started it all, you know. They
> produced all the doubt, they and the columnists in the *Wash-*
> *ington Post*, *The New York Times*, *Newsweek* and *Life*. And it
> spread and it spread until it appeared as if the people were
> against the war. Then Bobby began taking it up as his cause
> and with Martin Luther King on his payroll he went around
> stirring up the Negroes and telling them that if they came out

into the streets they'd get more. Then the Communists stepped in. They control the three networks, you know, and the forty major outlets of communication. It's all in the FBI reports. They prove everything. Not just about the reporters but about the professors, too. (p. 316)

After more remarks on the Communists' influence on the press and influential Americans:

Isn't it funny that I always received a piece of advice from my top advisors right after each of them had been in contact with someone in the Communist world? And isn't it funny that you could always find Dobrynin's car in front of Reston's house the night before Reston delivered a blast on Vietnam? (p. 317)

In 1967 the White House was beginning to be a grimmer and grimmer place, as Johnson struggled to maintain his dual projects of providing guns for "his" armies and butter for "his" people. As Lady Bird Johnson wrote in her January 1967 diary entry: "A miasma of trouble hangs over everything" (p. 508). Johnson once again was unsuccessful in talking Ho Chi Minh into initiating discussions about peace without the United States offering a halt in the bombings. Bobby Kennedy had captured the headlines with a plan for peace he had discussed with the French in Europe.

And then high officials in Johnson's administration began to flee the sinking ship. McGeorge Bundy left to head the Ford Foundation, aides Horace Busby and Jack Valenti left to go into private law practice and the Motion Picture Association, and then Bill Moyers left. He was a "son" of Johnson; perhaps his most trusted confidant. When he left to join *Newsweek* in February 1967, his departure became a catalyst for hatred. Suddenly stories began to circulate about his further blackening the President's name with his behind-the-back stories of

Johnson's cruelty (Turner, 1985). Then, in 1967, came reports of further dissension within the ranks: Robert McNamara and McGeorge Bundy, two of the original Vietnam hawks, had both given interviews objecting to escalation of the war, especially of the air war. In fact, it was during the hectic summer of 1967 that McNamara commissioned *The Pentagon Papers* (Turner, 1985).

As that tumultuous year ground on, Johnson, in response to a host of media and academic critics, was moved to speak on September 29 at San Antonio and announce the so-called San Antonio formula: "The United States is willing to stop all aerial and naval bombardment of North Vietnam when this will lead to productive discussions" (Turner, 1985, p. 196).

Finally, at the end of 1967, Robert McNamara himself left to head the World Bank. It is significant that the media, now arrayed against Johnson in full force, immediately spread a story that Johnson "dumped" him and had told the 107 world representatives of the Bank of his nomination of McNamara *before* he told McNamara (Turner, 1985, p. 207).

Johnson had been isolating himself for some time by confining his confidences to a trusted few. He had "rid himself" of the doubters—Bundy, Ball, Moyers—and now restricted his confidences to Rostow, Rusk, and others in the Tuesday conference committee. This system of demanding consensus and denying dissent in the Johnson entourage was described in several sources (Cooper, 1970; Reedy, 1970). As Kearns describes it:

> Once Johnson started on one of his monologues, it was difficult to halt him. If one of the listeners interrupted, trying to pull him back to the business at hand, he would become enraged. Yet if the listeners acquiesced by a smile or a sympathetic nodding of the head, Johnson's vanity proved unappeas-

able. The constant encouragement he demanded deadened the critical faculties of those still allowed access, creating a vacuum around himself and making him a prisoner of his own propaganda. Screening out options, facts, and ideas, Lyndon Johnson's personality operated to distort the truth in much the same way as ideology works in a totalitarian society. (p. 322)

And, of course, he received very little restraint or dissent from the Congress, who could have stopped the war at any time by rejecting the authorization bills for the Department of Defense to continue supplies for the war, or passed a bill requiring the President to stop the bombing (Evans & Novak, 1969).

Thus it was that Johnson—whose conduct as a president was so influenced by the overwhelming desire to maintain secrecy and protect against disclosure that would evoke criticism—was defeated by his inability to achieve genuine consensus with the country, his colleagues, and his advisers through disclosures that would have afforded him the support necessary to pursue a national policy where lives and families were at stake. All these decisions made to maintain his self-integrity could not be effective to provide for the legitimate needs of the country whose draft-age children were its paramount concern; not the attainment of a niche in the annals of history for a leader who might have delivered Vietnam from the hands of the Communists.

Chapter 7

SUMMATION AND OVERVIEW
ON JOHNSON AS THE FAILED LEADER

In this psychological history of our thirty-sixth president, Lyndon Baines Johnson, we have synthesized the many selves of Johnson into a cohesive psychological portrait. With his exposed vulnerabilities and his towering gifts, the man went lonely and hungry to the end. The data we have examined make it clear that Lyndon Johnson was deficient in self-worth and self-calming, which never could be altered nor alleviated by any of the ordinary experiences of life.

A reminder of the resistance of the self to change comes through the descriptions of Lyndon in his "retirement" on the LBJ ranch. Retirement from the leadership of the nation it was; retirement to a self now accepting of caretaking and benevolent direction it was not. Johnson continued to maintain control of his ranch hands, his family members, and his aides working on his memoirs and on the LBJ Library. While maintaining control of his retirement empire, he continued to need to be mentioned, to seek out applause for whatever was available as the currency to obtain the recognition he craved. He cherished admiration for his livestock and the produce from the farms; he related countless anecdotes from the past to whomever was available at the ranch to listen and applaud. And, of course, Johnson still as ever avoided situations where he might receive rebuffs, which kept him close to the ranch after the presidency and away from angry students and other protesters, and those in his party who no longer honored him (Kearns, 1976). In observing his final days, it is clear that he could not alter his self patterns and curtail his energy output to establish harmony with his vulnerable myocardium; and so he seemed to be rushing madly to his death. An example of this retirement behavior is contained in the following discussion he had with his biographer, Doris Kearns:

> It's all been determined, you know. Once more I am going to fail. I know it. I simply know it. All my life I've wanted to enjoy this land. I bought it. I paid it off. I watched it improve. It's all I have left now. And then this rotten spring comes along as dry as any we've had in fifty years. Everything that could go wrong does go wrong. First, the rains don't come. Then the Ford motor pump breaks down. Then the parts we order to fix it are delayed. And still the rains don't come. And if we don't get our fields watered soon, everything will be spoiled. Everything. Why, those parts were ordered weeks ago. They should have been here long before now. I can't depend on anyone anymore.
>
> I couldn't sleep all night. Not a minute. I kept thinking about those pump parts and about the rain and about my fields. And I couldn't stand it. I must have those parts before the end of the day. I simply must. If I don't, everything's going to fall apart. Everything. Now let's see, it's eight o'clock here, that means nine o'clock in Cincinnati. I must get started. (p. 361)

We will now round off the findings of our psychological investigation of Lyndon Johnson: what he demonstrated to the world, the profile of his self; whence in his background did his unique behavior and strivings arise; what continued to determine the special tactics and strategies he employed in his present world.

THE OMNIPRESENT SELF OF LYNDON JOHNSON

Lyndon Johnson demonstrated to the world, to begin with, a larger-than-life figure who was quick in mind and behavior and who—unless it was to his advantage temporarily to suppress himself—dominated each conversation or meeting he entered. He was able with his mental abilities to comprehend swiftly and to execute mental operations even faster. From earliest childhood he showed great courage and perseverance. Whether it was in the service of winning all the games as a fourth grader or evoking maternal protectiveness by running away, Lyndon showed stamina and fortitude in exposing himself to danger to accomplish his self-aims. He demonstrated the same qualities to accomplish his self needs throughout his childhood and adolescence. Now it was in clamoring for attention in being a delinquent scholar and adolescent rebel; now it was running away to California as a sixteen-year-old to get caught again.

In so many of his involvements in life between himself and a person, or himself and the "public," Lyndon *became* the self seeking to make contact with a source of mirroring and capturing the applause or the concern, but always fraught with the anxiety of abandonment. Another experience, that of disappointment, might come at the end of an interpersonal encounter in which he would find himself unfulfilled. The backbreaking work of the first congressional campaign comes to mind as one of his most important voyages for approval and its end point, the exhaustion and dangerous refusal to get treatment for the acute appendicitis he suffered at the close of the campaign. After President Kennedy died, Johnson stepped into the national disarray and had the government apparatus running with efficiency in a short time, in fact surpassing Kennedy's record by far for legislation initiated and passed. However, at the end of his courageous and resourceful term as president, his fear of standing for office in 1964 was so intense he told his wife he was going to withdraw from the campaign for the presidency (Kearns, 1976). Thus he demonstrated once again that his wishes for recognition (mirroring) were always *fearful,* never experienced with the confidence that his appeal for approval would be granted.

Another aspect of his self-strivings, that of seeking a leader, was revealed in the manner in which he made contact with special men and women of leadership quality whom he pedestalized, then attempted to drain of their power. The list of "political daddies" is a lengthy one. From each he received a transfusion of their special gifts. He took from FDR, Senator Wirtz, Mister Sam Rayburn, Richard Russell, and so many others, as we saw, never fully adhering to their precepts whether of populism or the New Deal or becoming a full member of the Southern congressional caucus. The capacity to seem attached and then extricate himself for what seemed to the outsider greener pastures was part of Johnson's self, stemming as we have demonstrated from early disappointments with his caretakers who taught him that reliance on another for nurturing and guidance is dangerous.

And so Johnson, fueled by his self-deficits, showed to some his need to receive applause, to others his need to receive their instruction or favors or advice.

Another vital aspect of his self was his ever-present strategies and tactics to maintain control over his surroundings. As the identified leader in a relationship or in an institution, he could control those whom he had established as his targets of idealizing or those whom he wished to be his engines of applause. He could control, or attempt to control, their presence or their separations, the intensity of the relationship, and be able to maintain discreetness in his individual relationships, so that rivalry was kept at a minimum. Using these tactics, Johnson's strategies would work: No one would leave him, no one owned him, and no one would be jealous.

One tactic he employed which exemplifies Johnson's techniques for maintaining control in his ever-urgent world of human relatedness was to broaden the number of relationships in which he was "involved." The strategy that stimulated this tactic was, as noted, to keep himself a moving target, so that he would always retain control and no one would be his only or major source of worth, knowledge, and decision making, and be in a position to leave him empty. Checking with Fortas, after checking with Clifford, after checking with Rusk, on an idea originating with McNamara, would be his mode. Utilizing the same tactic, Johnson shared many "intimate" moments with a variety of people including Lady Bird Johnson, Judge Moursand, Abe Fortas, and Alice Glass (Kearns, 1976).

All of our data gathering allows us to render an empathic diagnosis of his self-deficits and self-strengths—a diagnosis which addresses itself not only to the manifest behavioral data which we have rounded up, but represents an attempt to approach the inner experience of the man. We are able to make this diagnosis of his inner experience—as a result of collating the repetitive occurrences of the self patterns we have described, the "seeking" and the "grabbing" patterns of the mirror-hungry and ideal-hungry man. Thus, we assert that the empathic diagnosis of Lyndon Johnson is of a self-worth deficiency. The outstanding characteristics of this self pattern are those that Johnson so clearly experienced and showed: the empty, lonely man, vulnerable to rebuff, hanging on to each idealized relationship for the particles of nurturance he needed yet maintaining an aloof posture, and caught up in episodes of loss of worth.

WHERE DOES IT COME FROM?
THE GENETIC POINT OF VIEW

A distinguishing feature of a historical study of a person from the psychological side is the necessary emphasis on the background experiences of the subject. The psychological historian attempts to ferret out the learning environment of his subject, especially the learning that takes place between the subject and their early caretakers. In later life, the subject may be found to be repeating ancient methods of adapting to an environment in which the strategies and tactics of the past are no longer adaptive. Thus, the psychological historian seeks patterns of behavior in the present which reflect the past, especially the past deprivations of caretaking which stifle growth and cause a fixation of the growth of the self. The behaviors and experiences occurring in the present of our identified subject are studied to demonstrate evidences of sensitivities and vulnerabilities reflecting lack of development in a certain area of the self, such lack of adequate stores of self-worth, the resultant of inadequate mirroring from the selfobject caretakers.

Johnson's fixations became prominent as a three- and four-year-old when he began his unique behaviors of his hungry self seeking a responding environment. We were led to the conviction that Lyndon as a two-year-old experienced a withdrawal of his mother's ministrations after she became pregnant with the next of his siblings. The deprivations of mirroring, together with the absence of adequate surrogate and/or compensating selfobjects and a central nervous system proclivity, ordinarily lead to a fixation of experience and behavior. The experience that gets "stuck" and does not go away is that of the eternal emptiness of the deprived infant and the need for an appropriate caretaker (selfobject) who will be able to fulfill a two-year-old's needs for attention. Similar considerations apply to the experience, which Johnson missed, of being with an idealized caretaker (an idealized selfobject), the consistent calming-soothing relief of an idealized parent. Here again the fixation which formed in reaction to the deprivation resulted in the repetitious experiences and behavior of reenactment (acting out) of the little boy's wish to be calmed and directed by a leader.

Reviewing the circumstances of the life of Johnson, the depth psychologist's attention is drawn to the deprivation of mirroring and the lifetime esteem problem in Johnson which fueled so much of the behavior as a child, adolescent, and young and older man. As previ-

ously described, there were no associated parental surrogate figures who could be of service to Johnson.
Johnson was also not fortunate in his interactions with
potential sources of idealized parent supplies. Both Sam
Ealy Johnson, Sr. and Sam Ealy Johnson, Jr. were unable
to serve young Lyndon as compensation for his self-
esteem needs. The deprivation-to-fixation sequence in
this sphere led Johnson to be at the mercy of his ideal-
hungry self all his life; but, of course, never to relin-
quish control and again be at the mercy—as he would
experience it—of his critical male parent. Thus, Johnson's selfobject transferences were always in part *defense*
transferences, in which he maintained a psychic barrier
against total unfolding of his self-needs.

WHAT IS IT DOING HERE NOW?
THE LIFE OF SELF-REPAIR

Lyndon Johnson's life was in large part devoted to
self-repair, i.e., to the accretion of experiences that
would enhance his always hungry self-of-need. However, we are reminded immediately that his capacity totally to unfold to anyone did not allow for the human
bonds to form in sufficient depth to assure him the selfobject gratifications that he was seeking. And so his
adult life was often filled with instances of abortive
attempts to fill his self, only to be again disappointed—
by his own, albeit unconscious, fears of the self of re-
ceptivity required to ingest the supplies of mirroring
and calming sufficient to establish intrapsychic peace.

When Lyndon started out to form a relationship
with a significant figure, such as his wife, it was not
possible for him to make the plunge and form the love

bond that would ensure the needed selfobject gratifications. Suddenly, he was compelled backwards in psychological time, once again into the defense
transference of establishing the wall against the purveyors of worth, so as not to be vulnerable to their possible inconstancies or abandonment. Every relationship
he attempted to form was prone to these Sisyphean
mechanisms of inhibition. Lyndon's romantic encounter
with Lady Bird was intruded on by this same mechanism. His courtship was impassioned, as was the marriage, performed in the typical breakneck style of a
Johnson-engineered project. However, as Caro related
after his interviews with Mrs. Johnson, shortly after their
wedding, the heat of romance was gone and she was
shocked to hear the transference behavior—unrecognized by her—of Lyndon talking to his mother through
her (Caro, 1983). All of a sudden, the man so enthusias-
tic to form a love bond with her had pulled away, to
become an order-giver, a demander of her *total* devotion
to *his* missions; his capacity to unfold had been reached.
Proceeding further with the in-depth attachment of love
was impossible. Lady Bird had become, in Johnson's
experiences, mother Rebekah, and he could no longer
be receptive to "her" ministrations. He had again entered into his resistance against any and all purveyors of
self supplies, the defense transference. In Johnson's
case, we have surmised that his defense was originally
established to ensure against his being exposed to interminable and futile waiting for his mother—so caught up
with so many children—to respond.

In the same way, the self repairs that Johnson attempted to effect with his "daddies" could not and did
not ever come to fruition. He attempted to set on a
guru's throne a succession of men (and perhaps one

woman) whom he could idealize, bond with, and then follow. However, once again, as in his attempt to secure mirroring, his efforts were disturbed by the intrusion of the ancient resistance to allowing himself to be subservient. None of his attempts to establish a bond with a leader and interiorize the precepts of the leader could be realized. At the end of each unconsummated contract with a potential "daddy," he was searching to acquire another with whom he could relate. He could go just so far in opening himself up to a Richard Russell but then, as with all of his potential gurus, he would leave that club and proclaim his independence, and "be his own man." However, viewing his many attempts, and the gusto with which he entered into his attempts through the years to attain a guru–apprentice relationship, it was *not* that Johnson had to be his "own man" but that he pulled himself back from the full identification with his potential leaders and their precepts. This retreat was to the fixation process with which he was afflicted, continually reviving the fear of total exposure and everanticipated disappointment. No one owned Lyndon Johnson.

While it is true that Johnson did not achieve genuine intrapsychic peace and to the end of his days showed the symptoms of the narcissistically deficient person with loneliness and sensitivity to rebuff, he did achieve a significant measure of self-cohesion. Even with all the data that we have amassed revealing his difficulties, it certainly remains that Lyndon Johnson achieved considerable success in his political career. He managed to stay in psychological equilibrium sufficient to perform on an extremely high level for long periods of time over many years. Only when his self-repair activities failed, only when he could not achieve a balance of esteem and calming, or when he experienced a more precipitous rupture between his self and his selfobject world did Johnson undergo self-fragmentation. Thus, for example, he became fragmented when the world around him turned on him with hatred in reaction to the war in Vietnam. We now consider some episodes of self crises in Johnson's life.

In the case of the events after he became vice president, Johnson's narcissistic balance with his environment was disturbed and he experienced a loss of esteem sufficient to usher in a protracted period of depression. The loss of the leadership position he had held as a majority leader amounted to political death; but, more importantly, a precipitous loss in self-worth. He told Doris Kearns (1976) he felt he would "simply shrink up" (p. 160). He had tried to buttress his flagging self-worth through becoming the chairman of the Democratic Conference of the Democratic Conference of Senators, even though he was vice president. This tactic was defeated by the Democratic senators who knew it was an intrusion by the executive branch into the legislative branch of government (Evans & Novak, 1966).

He tried other tactics to elevate his status, including attempts to become a policymaker within the White House by asking President Kennedy to have him supervise areas of the government ordinarily overseen only by the president (Kearns, 1976). He became morose and withdrawn and uncharacteristically unresponsive even at the weekly White House breakfasts for legislative leaders (Schlesinger, 1965; Sorenson, 1965).

Johnson's profound loss of self-importance during his tenure as vice president demonstrated again his vulnerability to a change in his sensitive balance of esteem. Since his endogenous sources of esteem were never adequate to maintain self-cohesion, the need on his part to maintain the stream of applause from the outside world was always imminent. The world that gave him rewards as the majority leader was destroyed—John Kennedy, after all, was nine years his junior and a backbencher who just recently had petitioned Lyndon Johnson, when he was the Senate majority leader, to let his bills come up for passage (Schlesinger, 1965)—and thus was ushered in the experience of worthlessness.

The most profound reactions which Johnson experienced came with the protracted assaults on his self after the Vietnam war became a major conflict. So many people in so many institutions and of varied cultural and intellectual backgrounds rose up as one to assail Johnson. So many former colleagues deserted him and his position on the war. So many trusted cabinet members and friends ultimately abandoned him. Two of his most trusted advisors, McNamara and Clifford, finally went against him (Halberstam, 1972; Kearns, 1976; MacPhearson, 1972; Reedy, 1970).

Johnson's reaction was predictably a self-collapse, an acute and chronic fragmentation reaction which continued over several years. He did go through the anxiety states, the self-breakdown, with diminished reality testing and regressive outpourings of rage, with transient delusional states of persecution, which characterize such a self-collapse. How could he continue to hide the evidence of so many deaths on both sides? How could he hide the evidence of this in the cities and countryside in the foreign countries of Southeast Asia resulting from the actions of the war machine? How could he continue to hide the fact that the United States economy was faltering under the financial pressure of paying for the war and the Great Society? Thus, his failures at home and abroad were finally exposed. His fragmentation became more and more discernible to his staff, as his speech writer Richard Goodwin described (1988).

When Goodwin was drafting a speech on nuclear arms control for Johnson at the United Nations anniversary, Robert Kennedy, shortly before the United Nations anniversary, addressed the Senate in San Francisco and called for progress toward nuclear disarmament. It was a relatively minor address:

> But it infuriated Johnson, he called me in. "I want you to take out anything about the atom in that speech," he instructed. "I don't want one word in there that looks like I'm copying Bobby Kennedy." "But, Mr. President," I protested, "the Kennedy speech is very different from yours, and it's only his opinion. These are formal proposals from the President of the United States. The entire world will be listening." Johnson paid no attention; it was as if I hadn't spoken. He dropped his voice, picked up a newspaper. "Here's Reston's column on Kennedy's speech. You make sure we don't say anything that he says Bobby said. I'm not going to do it." Thus, all the arms control proposals were excised, the speech becoming little more than a banal birthday felicitations to the other members of the United Nations.
>
> Afterward, Johnson told Moyers, he would never use one word of the contaminated speech. In Goodwin's view, the American initiative toward instituting policies toward control of arms was never put in place because Kennedy had beaten Johnson to the idea. (p. 397)

Goodwin described another instance of Johnson's fears at this interchange:

> On June 28, I recorded in my diary that Johnson had asked me and Bill if we thought Tom Wicker was out to destroy him, if Wicker was caught up in some sort of conspiracy against him. We said no, that he writes some favorable and some unfavorable stories, but we couldn't convince him. Then he suddenly switched the subject to say he thought Bobby

Kennedy was behind the public assassination of Ed Clark—
whom he had made ambassador to Australia. Without waiting
for any reply, he went on to say that he had agreed to appoint
Harlan Cleveland to the number-four job in the State Department but now he wouldn't appoint him dogcatcher because he
thought he leaked the story to Reston about the U.N. Speech.
(p. 401)

A final quote from Goodwin's description of Johnson's unrest is as follows:

I'm not going to be known as the President who lost
Southeast Asia. I'm not going to be the one who lost this form
of government. The Communists already control the three major networks and the forty major outlets of communication.
Walter Lippmann is a Communist and so is Teddy White.
And, they're not the only ones. You'd all be shocked at the kind
of things revealed by the FBI reports. (p. 404)

The experience of self-enfeeblement leading to the
fears of persecution was contained in interviews Doris
Kearns (1976) conducted with LBJ:

"I felt," Johnson said, "that I was being chased on all
sides by a giant stampede coming at me from all directions. On
one side, the American people were stampeding me to do
something about Vietnam. On another side, the inflationary
economy was booming out of control. Up ahead were dozens
of danger signs pointing to another summer of riots in the
cities. I was being forced over the edge by rioting blacks, demonstrating students, marching welfare mothers, squawking
professors, and hysterical reporters. And then the *final straw.*
The thing I feared from the first day of my Presidency was
actually coming true. Robert Kennedy had openly announced
his intention to reclaim the throne in the memory of his
brother. And the American people, swayed by the magic of the
name, were dancing in the streets. The whole situation was
unbearable to me. After thirty years of public service, I de-
served something more than being left alone in the middle of
the plain, chased by stampedes on every side." (p. 347)

The self-enfeeblement was marked in this dream he related to her:

> In the dream he saw himself swimming in a river. He was swimming from the center toward one shore. He swam and swam, but he never seemed to get any closer. He turned around to swim to the other shore, but again he got nowhere. He was simply going round and round in circles. The dream reminded Johnson of his grandfather's story about driving the cattle across the river, where they, too, got caught in a whirl, circling round and round in the same spot. (p. 347)

The tragic self of Lyndon Johnson was now unmistakably revealed; he had no inner resources to fight off his "enemies." The "enemies" that initiated the self-collapse of LBJ were the original caretakers of his childhood, now revived in his inner self by the massive rebuffs of his critics.

Could or should a Lyndon Johnson with all the imbalances in his self lead our nation? We submit that the self-pathology of LBJ precluded this sensitive and unstable man from becoming an authentic leader of men. He could not perform what is in our view the elemental mission of a leader of a democracy—the demonstrated capacity to empathize with the elemental needs of the nation for the protection of the lives of their family members; and then to utilize the data of such empathic cognition in his decision making.

A tragedy such as the Vietnam war should not be recounted simply as a lesson of history; it should be blazoned in our books as a chilling example of the disasters overtaking the world when flawed leaders are given command of the engines of war.

Chapter 8

EPILOGUE

ON THE EMPATHIC APPROACH
TO CHOOSING A LEADER

We have attempted in this book to convey the central findings of the psyche of Lyndon Johnson which we uncovered after examination of the significant documents of his early life and his activities throughout his public life.

The self-deficits of Lyndon Johnson—the ceaseless need for approval and the corollary fear of loss of self-worth—were the central determinants in the decisions he made throughout his life and during his tenure as the thirty-sixth President of the United States. As president, whether the decision was made to initiate the programs of the Great Society or to enter into the Vietnam war or to halt the bombing of North Vietnam and enter peace negotiations, Johnson's self-deficits were ever present. These self-deficits—centered on his fear of the exposure of ineptitude—required him to be ever-vigilant to situations and people that might prove to be injurious to his self-worth and fostered decisions made solely to protect or enhance his self-worth.

Thus, Johnson as President was constantly at war with the Congress, the media and the press attempting to win in whatever combat he entered, since his self-worth was always on the line should he lose power and control and enter into what was for him the dreaded subservience (Chapter 4). We will now survey what we had adduced from the data we have gathered.

The first question of our research protocol is: What did Johnson demonstrate to his world of colleagues and intimates and casual observers? To this inquiry, we have described the following. Johnson had a constant fear of "someone" exposing his or any member of his entourage's ineptitude. Johnson had a single-minded concentration in any and all encounters on his self-issues. Whatever he was involved in would be the topic on which he would begin and end his "interpersonal" encounters. Another important finding revealed by the describers of the Johnson self was the undeveloped capacity for attention to others and identification with others, putting himself in the place of others (empathy). Johnson's experiential world consisted in the main of seeking out activities or people that would provide him with instant mirroring; and, gathering strength from senior mentors or other guiding figures such as Sam Rayburn, the great leader of the House of Representatives.

However, his drive to gain instant applause and his ability to engage in mentorship arrangements with "daddies" and "mommies" and his attempts to *own* people—all these unconscious attempts to gain supplies of self-love failed. Lyndon Johnson was a lonely person from his childhood to the end of his days. His death also occurred when he was alone in pain on his ranch.

Our next area of study of Lyndon Johnson was to the origins of his self. We adduced from the documents and from his manifest fears, sensitivities, and many other signs and symptoms of parental selfobject deprivation, that Johnson had missed significant experiences that would ensure a lifetime of self-calm and self-regard.

The final research item in our protocol attempted to gain insight into the manifestations of Johnson's past in the present. Johnson's repeated attempts to gain relief in so many of his adult relationships from the tension of his intrapsychic longings for succor, calming, and direction we have adduced, reflected his unconscious infantile and childhood and adolescent needs, "stuck," so to speak, both in terms of the archaic nature of the need and the archaic manner in which Johnson sought out and derived his gratifications. These latter observations lead us to the activities of Johnson as he initiated and maintained and refused to end the Vietnam war. These activities were pathognomonic of his narcissistic deficits in general and pathognomonic of the specific archaic tactics he utilized to garner those self supplies. The three phases of the war can be separated for our purposes so as to discern the psychological involvement of Johnson in each of these phases.

The initial entry into the war at Tonkin Bay came about as a decision based in large measure on Johnson's self needs. His needs at that time were to ensure a victory at the polls in the 1964 presidential contest with Barry Goldwater, the superpatriot and hyperassertive senator. Johnson's lunging at the opportunity to show his mettle both by retaliating with little evidence of being "unprovokedly attacked," and secondly by passing the Tonkin Bay Resolution, revealed his self-needs at that moment—to ensure himself against criticism for being soft on Communism, and to secure mirroring for being a combatant against Communism.

The second phase of the Vietnam war, opening in February 1965, came about through the bombing program unleashed against the forces of North Vietnam. Now Johnson and his advisers discarded the intent of the Tonkin Bay strictures of supporting the South Vietnamese government sufficiently for it to maintain cohesion against the advances of the Communist North Vietnamese. Johnson, over a short time, mounted a military force to search and destroy, i.e., to win a military victory and be the president who triumphed (unlike Truman in China) in Southeast Asia over Communism.

Finally, in this résumé of Johnson's self-states and self-needs, witnessed during the tragedy of the Vietnam war, we came to the resistance he displayed in halting the bombing and allowing the peace negotiations to proceed. Even as his Secretary of Defense Clark Clifford was exhorting him to give up bombing, even as he knew that Hubert Humphrey would be at a disadvantage in his presidential race with Richard Nixon if the peace negotiations were delayed, he would not stop the bombings. All observers agreed that Ho Chi Minh would not engage in negotiations unless the bombings stopped. It was clear that *Johnson* continued to want to win *his* war.

As Harry McPherson (1972), aide and speech writer, recorded of this hectic time: "...the extensive help which the president might have given Humphrey during the campaign was missing" (p. 443). As he reflected on his memories of Humphrey's chances for a victory fading away, since the negotiations for peace never were initiated, McPherson (1972) wrote "For Humphrey and for many of us in the White House, it was a bitter time" (p. 443).

The survey of the self states of Johnson as they were revealed in the Vietnam war confirms our assertion that the decisions he made to begin the war and be unable to end it were a reflection of his self-deficits. Johnson's decisions in this tragic war were not motivated, in our view, by empathic consideration for the lives of the soldiers and their families on either side; nor were his decisions motivated by the fears and hopes that ruled the minds of his fellow Americans. His decisions were fueled by self-needs which continued to direct him, albeit unconsciously, to seek out remedies to obtain gratifications for his appetites for mirroring and direction.

Freud's description (1939) of the leader/great man also included indifference to the needs of the masses who followed and revered the leader:

> ...a great man influences his fellowman in two ways: by his personality and by the idea which he puts forward...in the mass of mankind there is a powerful need for an authority who can be admired, before whom one bows down, by whom one is ruled and perhaps even ill-treated...it is a longing for the father. The decisiveness of thought, the strength of will, the energy of action are part of the picture of a father—but above all the autonomy and independence of the great man, his divine unconcern which may grow into ruthlessness. (pp. 109–110)

Kohut's views on the leader (1977) and his followers were that there were two major types of leaders exhibiting two selfobject functions which were of service in initiating or maintaining the cohesion of the masses or the group self, as Kohut described the group which coalesced out of a common self-need. As we have noted, the two types of leaders were the charismatic type and the messianic type, each exhibiting respectively the qualities of certitude and perfection (the charismatic leader) or the qualities of rectitude and the exalted self-esteem of the great man (the messianic leader) who led the way.

In Kohut's view, the group self needs had to be matched by a particular type of leader who could match the group self need at that point in time; in order to secure and maintain equilibrium, in effect to establish a group self/selfobject bond. Such was the case in the British group self's need in World War II for a charismatic leader who—as Churchill did—invited his people to merge with his grandiosity. Such was the case in the German nation after World War I whose group need was for a massive figure who would lead the people out of ignominy and poverty. They found their delivery in Adolf Hitler.

Kohut also made the point that as the group self needs changed after the particular economic or social crisis had passed, so did the need for a particular selfobject leader. Thus, at the end of World War II, Churchill, whose charismatic leadership was no longer appropriate to the needs of the group self of the British, was discarded (Muslin, 1985).

Lyndon Johnson's leadership, directly after the assassination of John Kennedy, prevented national disarray by his firm, controlled direction of the government. He exemplified the idealized leader *working in harmony* with the group self needs at that moment in history.

Perhaps more prominently in democratic states is the requirement of leaders to exhibit more awareness—empathic awareness—of the group self needs, and although our democracy at a quarter of a billion persons harbors many enclaves of special interest, there is a commonality of values of our leaders. One shared value in our society is that the president maintain a high level of decorum in manner and attitude. Another value of our president is that he is to be mindful of economic and social injustice. Yet another value we hold important is that the president is to value human lives and be mindful of the pain and the anguish to the survivor members of those families whose members may have perished in the defense of our country. Thus, a president who would enter into a conflict in which lives are at stake is expected to take this matter with the utmost forethought and foreplanning—what piece of land is at stake or what villainy is it sufficiently necessary to eradicate to expose lives, especially young lives, to danger or death?

Lyndon B. Johnson, as leader of the country, reflected in the specific decisions he took especially on the Vietnam war, cannot be said to have been in harmony with the known values of his country.

Johnson forced Congress to push through a Declaration of War against North Vietnam—the Tonkin Bay Resolution—acting in the guise of patriotism. Sacrificing lives to protect the flag or to maintain the honor or safety of the nation is an old and accepted value in this country. Sacrificing lives to show the nation that the leader is a superpatriot who would fight Communism at all costs is not an accepted, is even a dishonorable position.

Maintaining an unpopular war while large segments of our students were protesting on campuses, in the streets, at the Pentagon, represented an absence of empathy approaching indifference to the country's outcry.

Maintaining a secret government, which the journalists began calling Johnson's "credibility gap," which

encompassed a secret budget for the military, and keeping secret the number of war casualties represented an
absence of empathy on Johnson's part approaching indifference to the country.

Continuing the bombing of Vietnam after announcing that he would enter peace negotiations with the entire country, and with most of his cabinet and aides
against it—Fortas and Rusk the only exceptions in his
inner circle and, not coincidentally, the only survivors of
his original crew—represented perhaps the ultimate
self-centered decision making in his long history of sol-
ipsistic decisions made for the ostensible "good of
the people." Johnson did not take advantage of opportunities to stop the engines of war and the chance to
protect lives and families. His naked motivation was to
continue and maintain his chances to secure a victory in
Vietnam.

Johnson's decisions as the identified leader, and
hence his leadership, were not merely flawed, they were
not decisions befitting a leader of a democratic nation.
Was he simply not making a good fit between his self
and the group self, his *value* of winning a war against
Communism not in tune with the American public
group self values? It seems clear from the data we have
gathered and described that Lyndon's self needs based
on his self deficiencies did not permit empathic involvement with the "other" party, were the other party a single person or a group self. Therefore, he could never be a
leader if this term signifies a bond or fit between the
leader with a group or group self—his values shared
with the group self's values, his self merging with the
group self. Neither could he be a charismatic leader like
Churchill and invite his minions to share in his grandiosity; nor was he successful as a Moses-type leader, a

messianic figure proclaiming *the* pathway to a promised land and urging his flock to follow him.

Lyndon Johnson could not be a genuinely empathic selfobject to anyone. He was fixed onto the self of the mirror-hungry and the ideal-hungry child. Undeveloped as this fixated self was, the capacity for empathy never evolved to the point of the ability to extend fully himself into the other's self. Therefore, the ability to diagnose the other person's self state and gratify *their* wants in an act of genuine humanism based on an empathic diagnosis of *their* needs was missing in the self of Lyndon Johnson.

Here at the conclusion of our study of Lyndon Baines Johnson, the tragic self of Johnson can be seen with more clarity, as can the impact of this self on the country as he initiated and maintained and could not end the Vietnam war. The tragic self of Johnson—the unfulfilled though ever-clamoring, perpetually lonely persona—we have examined in sufficient depth to show his deficits and strengths and his inability to be a genuine leader of the country.

The intent of this book has been to demonstrate the values of a psychologically in-depth study of the man who so influenced hundreds of thousands of lives engaged in combat and millions of lives who were concerned and frightened spectators of the tragic events of the world in the 1960s and 1970s. One such value in our view is that it establishes the necessity for arriving at a diagnosis of the selves of those who stand for election as leaders of the country or other important positions in the national or local governments prior to the time of casting votes for or against their candidacy.

To the extent that we have demonstrated the value of an in-depth study of Johnson in becoming alerted to the ubiquitous problem in electing capable people to lead, our mission is completed. However, we are aware that the problem is complex and unending. How to enable reasonable people to become aware in sufficient depth of the personality of leaders to be elected so as to make an empathic diagnosis of their capacities for the type of leadership that will reflect the needs of the nation? Perhaps the more important question is, how do we set out to stimulate people to investigate in greater depth the data that will reveal the selves of our potential presidents?

In partial answer to the initial query, the unremitting trend of the media in this country and in the world is toward more and more disclosure of events and statements by candidates and leaders that reveal important diagnostic data of the selves of the candidates. At this writing, the media have uncovered or reported on events such as the sexual scandal of a Japanese prime minister; the disclosure of unheard-of financial rewards given for spurious reasons to congressmen; financial rewards given for influence-peddling to a former Secretary of the Interior, and many other events unreported to the nation and the world as recently as one generation ago. The media now represent in great part a genuine investigative body to which candidates must present their credentials for leadership and which now function as our collective watchdog and town crier, exhorting us to become enlightened observers.

Our final question represents a jeremiad of sorts: Why have we not made use of the views and tools of depth psychology and self psychology in choosing our future leaders? As can be seen in this study of Lyndon Johnson, the media and press now report in sufficient detail the material needed to form a psychological profile of the candidate for office. It remains for the observers, the nation at large, to round up the data to form an assessment of the self-functions necessary to evaluate the candidate's probable capacity for leadership. Does this candidate possess the empathic capacity for recognizing the varied concerns of the group: our social concerns, our economic concerns, our concerns about foreign affairs. Of course, much can be learned from the media reporting the candidate's record in his former positions, so that we are informed of the positions he has taken on a variety of national and international concerns. We need to hear the candidates interact in debate to know of their fund of knowledge and wisdom and their social concerns. There is often sufficient data to form an assessment of another self function, the capacity of the self to be resistive or to be vulnerable to self-fragmentation under stress.

Yet another aspect of the self necessary to evaluate is the candidate's endogenous store of self-worth or self-calming in contrast to his needs to secure mirroring or guidance from the surround. Does the candidate alter his views with different audiences to secure approval or does he maintain his firmly held convictions with each audience?

Finally, this book has attempted to contribute to the understanding of the psyche of a political leader and his impact on the world, and to demonstrate a method of study and inquiry to apply in assessing future candidates for leadership. Our hope is that our future leaders might be chosen for their capacities to know us in depth and to lead us through an empathic taking into account of our concerns and of our needs.

REFERENCES

CHAPTER 1

Caro, R. A. *The years of Lyndon Johnson: The path to power.* New York: Vintage Books, 1983.

Evans, R., & Novak, R. *Lyndon B. Johnson: The exercise of power.* New York: Signet Books, 1966.

Goldman, E. *The tragedy of Lyndon Johnson.* New York: Knopf, 1968.

Johnson, S. H. *My brother Lyndon.* New York: Cowles, 1969.

Kearns, D. *Lyndon Johnson and the American dream.* New York: Harper & Row, 1976.

Kohut, H. *The analysis of the self.* New York: International Universities Press, 1971.

Kohut, H. *How does analysis cure?* Chicago: University of Chicago Press, 1984.

Mooney, B. *LBJ: An irreverent chronicle.* New York: Crowell, 1976.

Muslin, H., & Desai, P. "The tragic self of Mahatma Gandhi." In *The Leader,* C. Strozier & D. Offer (Eds.). New York: Plenum Press, 1985.

Steinberg, A. *Sam Johnson's boy: A close-up of the president from Texas.* New York: Macmillan, 1968.

CHAPTER 2

Berman, E. *Hubert.* New York: Putnam, 1979.

Christian, G. *The president steps down.* New York: Macmillan, 1970.

Davie, M. *LBJ, a foreign observer's viewpoint.* New York: Duell Sloan & Pierce, 1966.

Dugger, R. *The politician, the life and times of Lyndon Johnson.* New York: W. W. Norton, 1982.

Evans, R., & Novak, R. *Lyndon B. Johnson: The exercise of power.* New York: Signet Books, 1966.

Goodwin, R. *Remembering America: A voice from the sixties.* Boston: Little Brown, 1988.

Halberstam, D. *The best and the brightest.* New York: Penguin Books, 1972.

Johnson, L. B. *A White House diary.* New York: Holt, Rinehart & Winston, 1970.

Johnson, R. B. *A family album* (J. S. Moursund, Ed.). New York: McGraw-Hill, 1965.

Johnson, S. H. *My brother Lyndon.* New York: Cowles, 1969.

Kearns, D. *Lyndon Johnson and the American dream.* New York: Harper & Row, 1976.

Miller, M. *Lyndon.* New York: Putnam, 1980.

Mooney, B. *LBJ: An irreverent chronicle.* New York: Crowell, 1976.

Moyers, B. "Overview by Bill Moyers." In *The Great Society,* B. Jordan & E. Rostow (Eds.). Austin, Texas: University of Texas, 1986, pp. 77–80.

Murphy, B. A. *Fortas: The rise and ruin of a Supreme Court Justice.* New York: William Morrow, 1988.

Pool, W. C., Craddock, E., & Conrad, D. E. *Lyndon Baines Johnson: The formative years.* San Marcos: Southwest Texas State College Press, 1965.

Reedy, G. *The twilight of the presidency.* New York: World, 1970.

Steinberg, A. *Sam Johnson's boy: A close-up of the president from Texas.* New York: Macmillan, 1968.

Valenti, J. *A very human president*. New York: W. W. Norton, 1975.

White, W. *The professional Lyndon B. Johnson*. Boston: Houghton Mifflin, 1964.

CHAPTER 3

Bell, J. *The Johnson treatment: How Lyndon B. Johnson took over the presidency and made it his own*. New York: Harper, 1965.

Caro, R. A. *The years of Lyndon Johnson: The path to power*. New York: Vintage Books, 1983.

Conkin, P. *Big Daddy from the Pedernales*. Boston: Twayne, 1986.

Cormier, F. *The way he was*. New York: Doubleday, 1977.

Dugger, R. *The politician, the life and times of Lyndon Johnson*. New York: W. W. Norton, 1982.

Evans, R., & Novak, R. *Lyndon B. Johnson: The exercise of power*. New York: Signet Books, 1966.

Halberstam, D. *The best and the brightest*. New York: Penguin Books, 1972.

Johnson, P. *Modern times*. New York: Harper & Row, 1983.

Johnson, S. H. *My brother Lyndon*. New York: Cowles, 1969.

Kearns, D. *Lyndon Johnson and the American dream*. New York: Harper & Row, 1976.

Miller, M. *Lyndon*. New York: Plenum, 1980.

Sidey, H. *A very personal presidency*. New York: Atheneum, 1968.

Steinberg, A. *Sam Johnson's boy: A close-up of the president from Texas*. New York: Macmillan, 1968.

White, W. *The professional Lyndon B. Johnson*. Boston: Houghton Mifflin, 1964.

Wicker, T. *JFK and LBJ: The influence of personality upon politics*. New York: William Morrow, 1968.

CHAPTER 4

Caro, R. A. *The years of Lyndon Johnson: The path to power.* New York: Vintage Books, 1983.

Cormier, F. *The way he was.* New York: Doubleday, 1977.

Dugger, R. *The politician, the life and times of Lyndon Johnson.* New York: W. W. Norton, 1982.

Johnson, R. B. *The family album.* J. S. Moursund, (Ed.). New York: McGraw-Hill, 1965.

Kearns, D. *Lyndon Johnson and the American dream.* New York: Harper & Row, 1976.

Kohut, H. *The analysis of the self.* New York: International Universities Press, 1971.

Kohut, H. *The restoration of the self.* New York: International Universities Press, 1977.

Kohut, H. & Wolf, E. The disorders of the self and their treatment. *International Journal of Psychoanalysis* 59:413–425, 1978.

Muslin, H., & Desai, P. "The tragic self of Mahatma Gandhi." In *The Leader,* C. Strozier & D. Offer (Eds.). New York: Plenum Press, 1985.

Steinberg, A. *Sam Johnson's boy: A close-up of the president from Texas.* New York: Macmillan, 1968.

CHAPTER 5

Caro, A. *The years of Lyndon Johnson: The path to power.* New York: Vintage Books, 1983.

Dugger, R. *The politician, the life and times of Lyndon Johnson.* New York: W. W. Norton, 1982.

Evans, R., & Novak, R. *Lyndon B. Johnson: The exercise of power.* New York: Signet Books, 1966.

Johnson, R. (Baines). *The family album.* S. Moursund (Ed.). New York: McGraw-Hill, 1965.

Johnson, S. H. *My brother Lyndon.* New York: Cowles, 1969.

Kearns, D. *Lyndon Johnson and the American dream.* New York: Harper & Row, 1976.

Muslin, H. "Analysis terminable and interminable: On self/selfobject fixation." In A. Goldberg (Ed.) *Progress in Self Psychology.* New Jersey: The Analytic Press, 1989, pp. 143–167.

Steinberg, A. *Sam Johnson's boy: A close-up of the president from Texas.* New York: Macmillan, 1968.

CHAPTER 6

Caro, R. A. *The years of Lyndon Johnson: The path to power.* New York: Vintage Books, 1983.

Cooper, C. L. *The lost crusade: America in Vietnam.* New York: Dodd & Mead, 1970.

Evans, R., & Novak, R. *Lyndon B. Johnson: The exercise in power.* New York: Signet Books, 1966.

Goulden, J. *Truth is the first casualty: The Gulf of Tonkin affair and reality.* Chicago: Rand McNally, 1969.

Halberstam, D. *The making of a quagmire.* New York: Random House, 1965.

Hoopes, T. *The limits of intervention: How America became involved in Vietnam.* New York: David McKay, 1973.

Johnson, G. W. (Ed.). *The Johnson presidential press conferences* (Vol. 1). New York: Earl Coleman, 1969.

Kahin, G. McT. *Intervention: How America became involved in Vietnam.* New York: Anchor Press, 1987.

Kearns, D. *Lyndon Johnson and the American dream.* New York: Harper & Row, 1976.

Kohut, H. *The analysis of the self.* New York: International Universities Press, 1971.

McPherson, H. *A political education.* Boston: Little Brown, 1972.

Reedy, G. *The twilight of the presidency.* New York: World, 1970.

Sidey, H. *A very personal presidency.* New York: Atheneum, 1968.

Tuchman, B. W. *The march of folly, from Troy to Vietnam.* New York: Ballantine Books, 1984.

CHAPTER 7

Caro, A. *The years of Lyndon Johnson: The path to power.* New York: Vintage Books, 1983.

Evans, R., & Novak, R. *Lyndon B. Johnson: The exercise of power.* New York: Signet Books, 1966.

Goodwin, R. *Remembering America: A voice from the sixties.* Boston: Little Brown, 1988.

Halberstam, D. *The making of a quagmire.* New York: Random House, 1965.

Kearns, D. *Lyndon Johnson and the American dream.* New York: Harper & Row, 1976.

McPherson, H. *A political education.* Boston: Little Brown, 1986.

Reedy, G. *The twilight of the presidency.* New York: World Press, 1970.

Rostow, W. *The diffusion of power.* New York: Macmillan, 1972.

BIBLIOGRAPHY

Austin, A. *The president's war: The story of the Tonkin Gulf Resolution and how the nation was trapped in Vietnam.* Philadelphia: J. B. Lippincott, 1971.

Baker, L. *The Johnson eclipse: A president's vice presidency.* New York: Macmillan, 1966.

Ball, G. W. *The past has another pattern.* New York: W. W. Norton, 1982.

Bishop, J. *A day in the life of President Johnson.* New York: Random House, 1967.

Bornet, V. D. *The presidency of Lyndon B. Johnson.* Kansas City: University Press of Kansas, 1983.

Burns, J. MacG. (Ed.). *To heal and to build: The programs of President Lyndon B. Johnson.* New York: McGraw-Hill, 1968.

Charlton, M., and Moncrief, A. *Many reasons why: The American involvement in Vietnam.* New York: Hill & Wang, 1978.

Clinch, N. G. *The Kennedy neurosis.* New York: Grosset & Dunlap, 1973.

Cohen, W. I. *Dean Rusk.* Totowa, NJ: Cooper Square Publishers, 1980.

Fall, B. *The two Vietnams: A political and military analysis.* New York: Praeger, 1964.

Frankel, C. *High on foggy bottom: An outsider's inside view of the government.* New York: Harper & Row, 1968.

Geyelin, P. L. *Lyndon B. Johnson and the world.* New York: Praeger, 1966.

Green, G. N. *The establishment in Texas politics.* Westport, CT: Greenwood Press, 1979.

Halberstam, D. *The powers that be.* New York: Knopf, 1979.

Harwood, R., and Johnson, H. *Lyndon.* New York: Praeger, 1973.

Herring, G. *America's longest war: The United States in Vietnam, 1950–1975.* New York: Wiley, 1979.

Hoopes, T. *The limits of intervention.* New York: David McKay, 1973.

Johnson, L. B. *A time for action: A selection from the speeches and writings of Lyndon B. Johnson, 1954–64.* New York: Atheneum, 1964.

Johnson, L. B. Luncheon for General Westmoreland: Remarks of the President, General Westmoreland and Secretary Rusk. April 28, 1967, *Weekly Compilation Presidential Documents* 3:674–679, May 8, 1967.

Johnson, L. B. *The vantage point: Perspectives of the president, 1963–1969.* New York: Holt, Rinehart & Winston, 1971.

Kluckhohn, F. L. *Lyndon's legacy: A candid look at the President's policymakers.* New York: Devin-Adair, 1964.

Krock, A. *Memoirs: Sixty years on the firing line.* New York: Funk & Wagnall, 1968.

Lansdale, E. G. *In the midst of wars.* New York: Harper & Row, 1973.

Newlon, C. *LBJ: The man from Johnson City.* New York: Dodd Mead, 1966.

Papers relating to the President's departmental reorganization program: A reference compilation. Washington, D.C.: Government Printing Office, 1971.

Porter, G. *Vietnam: The definitive documentation of human decisions.* Vols. 1 and 2. New York: Earl M. Coleman Enterprises, 1979.

Public papers of the presidents of the United States: Lyndon B. Johnson, 1967. Washington, D.C.: Government Printing Office, 1968.

Redford, E. S., and Blissett, Marian. *Organizing the executive branch: The Johnson presidency.* Chicago: University of Chicago Press, 1981.

Schandler, H. T. *The unmaking of a president: Lyndon Johnson and Vietnam.* Princeton, NJ: Princeton University Press, 1977.

Scheer, R. *How the United States got involved in Vietnam.* Washington: Center for the Study of Democratic Institutions, 1965.

Schoenbaum, T. J. *Waging peace and war: Dean Rusk in the Truman, Kennedy and Johnson years.* New York: Simon & Schuster, 1988.

Seidman, H. *Politics, position and power: The dynamics of federal organization.* New York: Oxford University Press, 1970.

The Senator Gravel edition—The Pentagon Papers, Vols. 1–4. Boston: Beacon Press, 1968.

Sherrill, R. *The accidental president.* New York: Grossman, 1967.

Smith, M. D. *The president's lady: An intimate biography of Mrs. Lyndon B. Johnson.* New York: Random House, 1964.

Taylor, M. *Swords and ploughshares.* New York: Norton, 1972.

Thies, W. J. *When governments collide: Coercion and diplomacy in the Vietnam conflict, 1964–1968.* Los Angeles: University of California Press, 1980.

Tran, V. D. *Our endless war inside Vietnam.* Novato, CA: Presidio Press, 1978.

GLOSSARY OF
COMMON TERMS
IN SELF PSYCHOLOGY

THE SELF

The self, the core of our personality, is a collection of our unique experiences throughout life. These experiences, laid down to become the inner mental life, comprise the experience from our earliest childhood environment to the present of, among others, significant people and their action. Included in the total collection of experiences which make up the self are those of one's physiognomy, events in the past and present and a whole body of external activities which have now become imprinted into the self. The experience of the caretakers' (selfobjects) functions of approval and applause become *crystallized* into an abiding experience of self-worth, the so-called pole of ambitions. The experience of the idealized caretaker's (selfobjects) functions of calming and soothing and direction-giving becomes crystallized into the so-called pole of values. Yet another constituent of the self is an intermediate area of basic talents and skills that are activated by the tension that establishes itself between ambitions and ideals.

SELFOBJECT

Selfobject refers to the self's experience of a person or a physical object upon which the self is dependent for its self-esteem. The self experiences its selfobject as separate—an object—but also as fused with itself—similar to a part of one's body, thus the term selfobject. The contact between the self is fusion, or merger, implying a high degree of closeness. The self experiences some persons or things not only as unique beings but as instruments (selfobjects). As the self matures and becomes more cohesive, greater degrees of internalization decrease the reliance of the self upon selfobjects. Selfobjects are of two basic types: mirroring selfobjects, in which the self is praised, reflected, acknowledged, and promoted by the other; and idealizing selfobjects wherein the other serves as a source of calming and soothing and a source of power to which the self can adhere. Later in life this selfobject offers standards to serve as guides for behavior.

MIRRORING SELFOBJECT

A mirroring selfobject constitutes a positive feed loop between the self and the representation or so-called imago or inner experience of an authority figure, ordinarily a parent, who functions as an applauder, approver, admirer, the important support system of early infancy. In infancy this selfobject function is the major source of the infant's *experience* of being valued, thus the term archaic mirroring selfobject.

NARCISSISM

Narcissism refers to the self-love or self-worth or self-value of an individual. Narcissistic deficits are those of diminished self-worth, narcissistic excesses are grandiosity states.

FRAGMENTATION

When the selfobject abruptly ceases its function for the self, a process of restructuring takes place in which the economy of selfobject function for the narcissistic self is disrupted with such severity that primitive defensive processes, i.e., disavowal, denial, projection, and psychotic-like processes, i.e., reality breaches, confusion, severe dysphoria, and anxiety all occur for a period of time until a new constellation of selfobjects is deployed.

ARCHAIC SELFOBJECT

This refers to the earliest selfobject functions of mirroring (instilling worth) or being the idealized parent who calms and soothes. The internalization of selfobject function constitutes the inner core of the self. Thus the contributions of these archaic selfobjects to the self determine the richness and flexibility of the self that is being formed.

INTERIORIZATION OR INTERNALIZATION (TRANSMUTING INTERNALIZATION)

This is the process by which the functions of the archaic selfobjects, either to approve or to calm, become an actual addition to the contents of the self so that self-esteem—an intrapsychic function—replaces selfobject mirroring—an interpersonal activity. Internalization of selfobject functions, mirroring, or the functions of the idealized parent, take place along the lines first articulated by Freud in "Mourning and Melancholia" that describes the mourner's unique reaction to loss—internalization of significant aspects of the departed person—as an ubiquitous reaction to separation.

NARCISSISTIC HURT OR NARCISSISTIC INJURY

This is the condition that occurs when a self/selfobject bond becomes interrupted or ruptured, and is experienced by the self as a loss of regard, value, or worth. If a self–selfobject bond is ruptured precipitously, what often eventuates is an experience of massive anxiety (disintegration anxiety) followed by a fragmentation reaction. If a fragmentation reaction is severe various constituents of the self including reality testing and repression are disturbed and this results in a condition akin to psychosis, a brief minipsychosis or the surfacing of primitive defensive postures such as projection.

COHESIVE SELF

A cohesive self is that self in which internalization of the functions of the selfobjects have now been completed, and the self is now in a state of equilibrium or cohesion.

NUCLEAR SELF

Nuclear self is the self that is the resultant of the internalizations from the selfobjects of one's infancy and early childhood and thus represents the early form of the maturing self. This structure is bipolar in its psychological morphology, one pole representing the transformed archaic grandiosity into the pole of ambitions, the other pole representing the internalized archaic idealizations into the transformed pole of ideas. This early self has a pole of ambitions that strives to live up to its pole of ideals through the talents and skills of the self which are internalized through the self's identification with a parent who functions in a twinship merger.

OPTIMAL FRUSTRATIONS

Optimal frustrations refer to the unavoidable disappointments in child rearing such that the child does not obtain the instant feedback that he or she may be demanding. These unavoidable delays, absences, or misappreciations, which are not protracted or in any way traumatic (optimal frustrations), promote the internalization of the mirroring of other selfobject functions so that the child now has the mirroring selfobject's approval attached, so to speak, to his or her self as a permanent source of nurturance (transmuting internalization).

ARCHAIC SELF/SELFOBJECT RELATIONSHIPS

The earlier self/selfobject contacts, whether mirroring or idealized parenting, are actually merging types of relationships. They instill in the child esteem, or calming after optimal frustration and internalizations of the functions of the selfobject.

MATURE SELF/SELFOBJECT RELATIONSHIPS

From the archaic selfobject relationships there is a developmental line of self/selfobject encounters to the so-called mature selfobject relationships that offer an experience of empathic resonance—the admiration of a colleague, for example, to which the adult self can experience a revival of the memory traces of the archaic selfobject's mirroring or calming and soothing, and in this manner can restore a disequilibrium due to temporary flagging of esteem. Throughout one's development, the self requires occasional selfobject refueling to maintain the integrity of the self. At times the selfobject encounters will approach the approving, admiring, calming, soothing, merging interactions resembling the archaic self/selfobject fusions.

ARCHAIC GRANDIOSITY

An early stage of the infantile self, during which time the infant receives a large amount of mirroring, instilling in that infant the experience of total control over its environment.

ARCHAIC IDEALIZATION

An early stage of the infant's relationship with the idealized parent imago, an archaic self/selfobject encounter, ushers in the experience in the infant that the idealized parent selfobject is the omnipotent center of the universe.

GROUP SELF

At times in any culture, the group members bond together, especially in times of crisis, to become transformed into an entity that in many ways resembles an individual self; therefore the designation—group self. This group self, especially during times of crisis, is often in contact with or seeks out a leader who provides a selfobject function. Therefore, this interaction can be designated as a selfobject/group self dyad.

THE TENSION ARC OF THE SELF

In the adult self, the cohesion of the self is maintained through the tension arc created by the pole of ambitions striving to live up to the ideals through the exertions of talents and skills in what might be called a program of action.

OBJECT LOVE

The experience of the selfobject, as has been described, is the experience of an entity that performs a set of functions, either mirroring or idealized parenting, that instills in the self the ultimate experience of self-worth, or self-calming and soothing, or ideals and standards. A love object, however, is experienced by the self as a separate entity, with separate individual features, that does not perform any of the functions of mirroring or idealized parenting. Object love refers to the experience of valuing the significant other for their individual qualities, differentiated from selfobject love, which is an attachment behavior of someone who is attached to a selfobject for its particular functions performed for that self.

EMPATHY

Empathy refers to a process of vicarious introspection through which the observer determines the state of the self of the other at a point in time. This is a cognitive event independent of sympathy which is the emotional act of momentarily identifying with the other's self state or the awareness of experiences similar to those occurring in the self of the other.

NARCISSISTIC PERSONALITY DISORDERS

These are the disturbances in a precariously organized cohesive self with a tendency to temporary fragmentations when self/selfobject disruption occurs. The presenting symptoms are hypochondriasis, depression, hypersensitivity to rebuff, emptiness and loneliness, naughtiness, and the tendency to form archaic self/selfobject bonds.

INDEX